If you will take the teaching of this book ~~into~~ your life, then you and those around you will be on a remarkable journey of transformation and life! The principles that Tom teaches here are incredibly helpful and I personally have learned from them and seen them bear much fruit in leaders around me. If you want to be a leader who helps others to thrive and walk forward in their unique God-given identity and calling, then this is the book for you. Tom's wisdom and generous heart towards the body of Christ mean that his journey in all things to do with coaching is full of credible and godly insight. Read on and see change!

Nicola Bass, Senior Pastor, Life Vineyard Church, Newcastle, UK, and Coaching Coordinator, Vineyard UK and Ireland

Once in a while, someone comes along with something really life-changing. Tom has touched and changed the lives of many hundreds of people with his coaching. Now you can experience that life change with this book too. Learn how powerful coaching can be, how to engage in it and the transformation it can bring you. Any leader who wants to get more in touch with who they are and what they are called to be needs to read this book.

Dr Jason Clark, Visiting Professor, Portland Seminary, Oregon, USA, and Senior Pastor, Sutton Vineyard, UK

I love this book. It will definitely light some fires and save some lives that might otherwise be broken on the altars of ministry. Tom gets it. Most of God's investment in those we coach is buried under the dirt of everyday living.

The book is full of interesting stories of people not fully understanding the value of what's in front of them. These stories parallel my own experience both as an young man displaying little potential and later as a coach sometimes overlooking the gold in the life of another.

The book is a great coaching manual, and his argument for a 'sweet spot' is worth the price. It's also a good, fun read. You'll love it.

Coaching the gold can change our world.

Ralph Moore, founder, Hope Chapel movement, California and Honolulu, USA

Tom and I have got to know each other in a group of churches called the Vineyard. In our tribe, we have a saying, 'Everyone gets to play.' In Tom's book, *Mining for Gold*, that phrase comes to life as he helps us empower every person to come alive and take part in the game of kingdom ministry. There is treasure in every person who gathers in our churches every week. This book is a great tool to help us discover that treasure and develop leaders who come alive and thrive.
Jay Pathak, Lead Pastor, Mile High Vineyard, Denver, Colorado, USA

Tom has the heart of a true developer: he loves to see people raised up to become what God has made them to be, unleashed in their God-given design. He isn't just a leader who cares about getting things done; he cares about allowing people to flourish in God's plan for them. *Mining for Gold* draws on Tom's treasure trove of insight and experience in raising people up through coaching. Developing leaders is such a critical task for the future of the church, and there are priceless keys in this book.
Putty Putman, founder, School of Kingdom Ministry, Illinois, USA, and author of Live like Jesus *and* Kingdom Impact

I can barely think of a more critical skill for this current milieu of ministry than coaching. As accessible as it is gracious, Tom gives us a practical path to empowerment, taking us into the deepest possible waters of true servant leadership. I am so grateful for this book.
Brian Sanders, founder, Underground Network, and IVP author

Gold is a rare commodity of great value – mined and refined at great cost – and so is a good leader. Tom, in this practical leadership coaching book, reminds us of the importance of refinement in leadership. Fruitful, multiplying leaders are refined by God and shaped through intentional coaching. This book will help you practically to uncover six important principles of thriving leaders and is worth its weight in gold.
Ed Stetzer, Billy Graham Distinguished Chair, Wheaton College, Illinois, USA

MINING
FOR
GOLD

MINING
FOR
GOLD

Developing Kingdom
Leaders through Coaching

Tom Camacho

INTER-VARSITY PRESS
36 Causton Street, London SW1P 4ST, England
Email: ivp@ivpbooks.com
Website: www.ivpbooks.com

Bible acknowledgments can be found on page 184.

First published 2019

British Library Cataloguing-in-Publication Data
A catalogue record for this book is available from the British Library.

ISBN: 978–1–78359–932–5
eBook ISBN: 978–1–78359–933–2

Set in Dante 12/15 pt
Typeset in Great Britain by CRB Associates, Potterhanworth, Lincolnshire
Printed in Great Britain by Ashford Colour Press Ltd, Gosport, Hampshire

*Inter-Varsity Press publishes Christian books that are true to the Bible and that
communicate the gospel, develop discipleship and strengthen the church for its mission
in the world.*

*IVP originated within the Inter-Varsity Fellowship, now the Universities and Colleges
Christian Fellowship, a student movement connecting Christian Unions in universities
and colleges throughout Great Britain, and a member movement of the International
Fellowship of Evangelical Students. Website: www.uccf.org.uk. That historic association
is maintained, and all senior IVP staff and committee members subscribe to the UCCF
Basis of Faith.*

CONTENTS

FOREWORD

I write as one who has benefited significantly from being on the receiving end of coaching from Tom Camacho. I am, as a result, enthusiastic about what coaching could do both in your life and, through you, for others.

This book is a practical manual, written in an engaging, accessible and sometimes vulnerable way. There are helpful suggestions for application to your own life, and also to those you might coach yourself.

I love the simplicity with which Tom captures and unpacks some profound truths. On one level these concepts are not that complicated, yet they can be life-transforming when they are applied.

Take, for instance, the idea that thriving comes from living out of the way we were designed as individuals. It's much more enjoyable as well as productive if we are doing what we're good at. When we love what we do, we find energy we didn't know we had.

Tom explores how we might identify 'what we are for', and provides tools to help align that understanding with what we spend most of our time doing. The greater the alignment, the greater our effectiveness and fulfilment in life, relationships, work and ministry.

As the Apostle Paul wrote in his letter to the Ephesians, 'we are God's handiwork, created in Christ Jesus to do good works, which God prepared in advance for us to do' (2:10, NIV).

With the help of a coach, we can go a long way towards understanding how God made us and identifying which of our activities are those he has prepared for us to do. Most of us are probably doing some of the good works which God designed someone else to do. As long as we hold on to them, not only are we in danger of striving rather than thriving, but actually we could be denying someone else the opportunity to fulfil his or her calling.

Coaching is so helpful in that journey. It brings an objective perspective and draws out of the person being coached his or her own answers to the really pertinent questions. The coaching process gives rise to action points, and creates accountability to do something that contributes to tangible progress before the next coaching session.

In mentoring, the helper has to be further ahead in an area of relevant experience than the person being helped. A coach, however, simply needs to learn the skills of helping a person to reach his or her own answers and solutions. It can be hugely rewarding for both parties: the coach sees how valuable such work is to the person on the receiving end, and the one being coached finds breakthroughs in challenging areas.

Within our movement, many have benefited from this approach, and as we continue to train more coaches we are excited that the fruit we have seen so far will be multiplied.

I commend this book to you.

John Wright
National Director, Vineyard Churches, UK & Ireland

ACKNOWLEDGMENTS

The journey of writing this book has been a long process filled with many touches from the Father and his people. I want first to thank my beautiful wife, Beth, for dreaming with me, challenging me and stretching me to seek God's highest and best in everything. Your support and steady love are my anchor.

To Caleb and Andrea, Daniel, Caryn and Rebecca: I feel so grateful to have you in my life. You always encourage me to keep reaching and risking.

I thank Bob Logan, a true father in the coaching and multiplication realm, for personally mentoring and coaching me. Your skills and care as a coach unlocked me and my calling. This book would never have happened without your influence and example. Thank you from the depths of my heart.

To Michael Gatlin, Justin Juntinen and the Multiply Vineyard team: thank you for letting me be myself and encouraging me to share what God put in my heart.

I thank my dear friend Jason Clark for activating this book project in me and opening the door to it being written.

Thank you, Nicola Bass, for dreaming with us and cheering me on through this whole process.

To John and Debby Wright and all my friends from the Vineyard in the UK and Ireland: you received us and these principles with open hearts and minds. I am so grateful for your love and friendships.

Finally, to my great friend Steve Mitchell: you mined for the gold of this book in me. I respect and treasure your friendship and coaching in my life. Your team at IVP UK is fantastic and committed to the kingdom and to great publishing.

To God: thank you for making so many masterpieces and letting me have a small part in bringing them forth for your glory.

INTRODUCTION: GOLD

He will sit as a refiner and purifier of silver, and he
will purify the sons of Levi and refine them like gold
and silver, and they will bring offerings in
righteousness to the LORD.

Malachi 3:3, ESV

Thriving kingdom leaders are like pure gold. They are very valuable and they are quite scarce. Loving, fruitful and multiplying leaders are works of art, masterpieces fashioned by the hands of God himself. Like trees bearing fruit in season, their leaves don't wither and they fulfil the call God has for their lives. Look through the Scriptures and the pages of church history and you will see countless examples where God placed a deposit of gold in a person, called out that gold, and then began the slow and exacting process of refining that gold for his glory. God personally invited Moses, David, Esther, Peter and Paul as vessels into his gold-refining process, and he is inviting every one of us as well. God, the great Refiner, patiently transforms leaders until their hearts and characters beautifully reflect his own. He is a miner and a refiner of leaders.

The value of gold

Gold has been treasured by cultures all over the world since the beginning of time. God had Moses make the most precious articles of the tabernacle out of pure gold. Jesus counselled the Laodicean church in Revelation 3:18 to buy from him 'gold refined by fire'. Abraham and Solomon became very wealthy with great quantities of gold. John saw in his revelation that the streets of the heavenly Jerusalem were made of pure gold.

Of gold usage globally, 80% is used in the making of jewellery. Gold bars are held by large banks as reserves to guarantee their ability to repay depositors and trading partners. Gold is also used in coinage, medicine, dentistry, computers and even aerospace applications. And, of course, gold is used in making the highest Olympic medal. Gold is a universally accepted substance of the highest value. It is valuable for several reasons:

- *It is beautiful.* Its shimmering yellow colour is attractive and unlike any other mineral.
- *It is pure.* Gold has unique metallurgical properties. It does not corrode or rust. It does not bond easily with other minerals.
- *It is soft.* Gold is one of the most malleable substances on earth. A single chunk of gold can be made into a thin wire that stretches for miles.
- *It is rare.* Gold is very scarce. All the gold on the planet could fit into a cubed space the size of a tennis court!

Godly kingdom leaders are the same. They are precious, mouldable treasures called to serve as attractive representatives of the King of kings. Their hearts are soft and their love for God and others is tangible. God sees their great value, and we should too. They are precious because they reflect God himself and influence others in ways that build his kingdom. In my thirty-five years of leadership experience in the body of Christ, I have found that every church, missions group or Christian business would gladly welcome the precious resource of more godly leaders.

The gold of thriving godly leaders

Look more closely at Malachi 3:3. The sons of Levi were the priests, the leaders in the work of the tabernacle, the place where God met with man. In this verse God is saying he will develop thriving kingdom leaders after his own heart. The passage states that God sits, meaning he forever takes his place, as a refiner of leaders, personally working to purify them and prepare them to bring righteous offerings. Righteous offerings are the pleasant fruit of faithful service offered by Christian leaders to their King. As the Refiner, God works continuously to call and shape leaders so they bring pleasant offerings to him, and they bear the fruit he created them to bear. God never stops developing leaders. He is inviting us to join him in this exciting and important effort. Just as he used Paul and Barnabas to raise up godly, thriving leaders in every city (Acts 14:23), he wants to use us to raise up leaders in our local context. He does the work. He is the Refiner of gold and silver. We are simply invited to cooperate with him in this critical kingdom task.

Thriving, godly leaders are precious like gold but they also carry a treasure inside themselves (2 Corinthians 4:6–7). Each Christian leader carries a deposit of God's nature inside them through the new birth. The Holy Spirit, a member of the Trinity, lives inside them and flows through them. Paul called this gold in every believer 'Christ in you, the hope of glory' (Colossians 1:27). We carry the treasure of his image in our earthen vessels. We bear the image of God himself in our weak human condition. It is a miracle beyond comprehension that the God of the universe, the perfect, uncreated one, lives inside you and me. It's so incredible. Our unique wiring and personality, inflamed by the Spirit of God, are like a weight of gold on the inside of us. We are all valuable and unique sons and daughters of the God of all creation.

The mission of the kingdom around the world is in continuous need of a fresh supply of godly leaders. What would be possible if your church or ministry had an instant supply of twice the number of thriving leaders you have today? How could you make an impact on your community if you had a continuous new crop of thriving leaders to serve and bring forward your dream and vision? The possibilities are endless. The world needs more godly, thriving leaders.

This book is written to help in this vital process of identifying, moulding and shaping thriving kingdom leaders. We are called as leaders to mine for the gold in others, cooperate with God as he refines that gold and then help them invest that gold in the kingdom. We have the privilege of joining God as he shapes leaders for his life-giving kingdom work. We need to learn the skills and principles to do it well. Our role is to cooperate with him in his leader development process. He is the Refiner and he is inviting us to be his assistants.

Mining for Gold

I want to introduce you to the concept of **Mining for Gold**, a coaching style of leadership. In this book, I will use the terms 'Mining for Gold' and 'Coaching Leadership' interchangeably. Mining for Gold is a leadership paradigm that incorporates the best principles of Christ-centred coaching into our everyday practice of developing others. Mining for Gold/Coaching Leadership is a fresh way to look at leadership development. It is a Spirit-led process. The key components are simple, but they require hard work, sensitivity and focus to do them well. To help us understand and remember what Coaching Leadership looks like, I've formed an acrostic from the word GOLD.

Here are the four key concepts of Mining for Gold/ Coaching Leadership:

- *Gold is everywhere.* Potential leaders are all around you, waiting for someone to help them become who God created them to be. We are not victims of a scarcity of leaders. We need to see leadership development from an abundance mentality. Godly, thriving leaders are scarce, but the raw material for developing those leaders is everywhere.
- *Open your eyes to see it.* We do not see the gold around us because it is in such a raw, undeveloped form. We need to pray and ask God to open our eyes to see. To identify the true potential God has placed in leaders, we need to see them through the eyes of the Spirit.
- *Learn the skills to draw it out.* The skills of Mining for Gold are practical and learnable. We must commit ourselves and put in the hard work to learn the skills of Coaching Leadership, increasing our competency in developing leaders.
- *Develop others continuously.* Leader development must remain a high priority for us in our own leadership. One of our greatest contributions as leaders is to leave a legacy of godly kingdom leaders. We need intentionality and focus to continuously develop the leaders around us.

Thriving kingdom leaders are not a coincidence. They are the product of God's intentional loving care and development. He is forever developing them. As coaching leaders, we get to participate in the development of these precious leaders. Just as a tree needs the right setting and nutrients to grow and bear fruit, Christian leaders need certain conditions to truly thrive. Planted in good soil and nurtured by skilled coaching leaders, a crop of thriving godly leaders will emerge, just as a crop emerges when good seed is planted in good soil.

The six principles of Mining for Gold / Coaching Leadership

Here are six principles that are key in the development of thriving, godly leaders:

1. *The Holy Spirit does the work of refining.* He is in charge, not us. Our role is to learn to work in dynamic cooperation with him.
2. *Our true identity is the foundation of thriving.* We are beloved sons and daughters of a perfect Father and King. Any other foundation is false and will fail us.
3. *We thrive when we cooperate with our God-given design.* Something powerful happens when we align our time and efforts with how God wired us.
4. *Each of us has a sweet spot – a place where we naturally bear the most fruit.* Finding this place is like being set free from a cage. We have permission to be ourselves and thrive.
5. *The cross is God's great refining tool.* There is no escaping this painful reality. The great heat of the cross is God's primary tool in purifying thriving leaders.
6. *All true thriving is relational.* There is nothing more central than to love God and love others well. No achievement can take the place of thriving in our

primary relationships. The Trinity works in dynamic unity of relationships. We must join in that relational reality.

Take a journey with me to discover how to mine for gold in others. It is an exciting and dynamic path. It requires great discipline and focus. It is complex, but learnable. The fruit that awaits you will take your breath away. There is so much gold out there waiting to be discovered. Let me share a story to help illustrate this.

Gold!

The sun was high and warming up the fields on the Highveld, the mile-high plateau in north-eastern South Africa. It was February 1886 and summertime in the southern hemisphere. All across the Transvaal, groups of mineral seekers were scoping out the area, digging in the dirt and pursuing their fortune. These treasure seekers were after precious minerals, gold and diamonds, waiting to be found in the soil of this young British colony.

There had long been rumours of gold, even a city of gold, yet to be discovered in the region by some lucky fortune hunter. Nearly twenty years earlier, fifteen-year-old Erasmus Jacobs had found a large, clear stone along the Orange River near the town of Hopetown. Gemologists soon confirmed the stone as a pure diamond. Aptly named the Eureka Diamond, it is a humongous 24-carat crystal and the first recorded diamond discovered in South Africa. The Eureka Diamond is now a national treasure, belonging to the people of that country. Jacobs's discovery kicked off a flood of treasure seekers who descended on the region from all over the world.

Two British men, George Harrison and George Walker, were hungry for gold. Each man had a history of mining in their veins, Harrison in the gold fields of Australia, and Walker as a coal miner in England. They teamed up to seek a deposit of the valuable yellow substance. For some time, their focus had been in and around the Oosthuizen farm, near present-day Johannesburg. After months of searching, they had found nothing.

There is ongoing debate as to which man found the gold first. Harrison claimed he found it, but Walker said he did. These were Walker's words recorded in the *Sunday Times* in 1924, more than thirty-five years after the discovery.

> [In February 1886] I stumbled over an outcrop of rock and, on examining it, found it to be conglomerate [gold-bearing]. I became the prospector chipping a bit here, a bit there, of the rock. Then I took it to where we were building the house of Oosthuizen, where the house stands to this day . . . When I had crushed it as fine as I could get it, I found an old frying pan belonging to Mrs Oosthuizen. The result in the pan took my breath away. The bottom of the pan was covered with gold.

Regardless of who actually found the gold that day, the impact of their incredible discovery was explosive: changing the course of a nation, raising up the mighty city of Johannesburg, and inciting a war between the British and the Dutch as to who would control the minerals of South Africa. Walker and Harrison soon learned they had stumbled upon one of the greatest gold-producing deposits in world history: the Witwatersrand Gold Field.

The Witwatersrand Basin (Witwatersrand in Dutch means 'white water ridge') is a largely underground geological formation holding the world's largest known gold reserves. It has produced over 1.5 billion ounces (over 40,000 metric tons) of gold. That represents about 50% of all the gold ever mined on earth! For weeks, these two men from Great Britain had been walking on top of the greatest gold deposit the world would ever see. They just didn't know it!

As word of their discovery spread, thousands of gold miners from across the world filled the region almost overnight. Within two years, four mining companies had been established with the capital, engineering and technology to bring the gold out of the earth. The city of Johannesburg mushroomed in growth as merchants and traders sought to make money selling equipment and supplies to the miners. Eventually the Second Boer War was fought to determine which nation, the English or the Dutch, would have rights over the growing mineral riches coming out of the mines all across the region. The British eventually prevailed. The discovery of these precious minerals changed the course of history, not just in southern Africa, but across the world.

The treasure of godly leaders

The gold of leaders is out there, perhaps right under our feet, if we have eyes to see it. We need to hunger to discover the gold of godly kingdom leaders. We need to mine for it. When we look out across our churches, Christian ministries and kingdom businesses, we may see a landscape of people that seems pretty ordinary. These people are like the land on the Oosthuizens' farm. They appear unremarkable on the surface, but carry something incredibly valuable underneath. Where we see ordinary people, God sees something different. He sees within them a rich deposit of gold waiting to be brought forth. God sees leaders waiting to be discovered.

The gold inside God's people is vastly more valuable than any natural mineral the world has ever seen. Our task is to become gold miners, treasure seekers, who work continuously with God in the search and development of godly kingdom leaders.

The war over the treasure

Be informed. There is a battle over the gold of thriving, godly leaders. Whenever gold has been found in human history, there has often been a battle that ensues for the rights to control the wealth of that resource. It is the same with the gold of godly leaders. We have a real enemy, the devil, who wants to steal that gold and will fight the process at every turn.

> The thief comes only to steal and kill and destroy; I have come that they may have life, and have it to the full.
> (Jesus, John 10:10, NIV)

The devil does not want thriving kingdom leaders to be developed. He doesn't want godly leaders to thrive. He does not want Christ to be revealed. He works relentlessly to kill, steal and destroy the treasure God has placed within each person. But we have a Saviour, Christ Jesus, the Lord, who has won the war with our enemy! Jesus daily defeats Satan and his schemes, and will bring his leaders into a life of freedom and abundance (John 10:10). He calls leaders to come and discover his abundant life and thrive. He is a beautiful Saviour. He is saying, 'Follow me, and I will teach you how to thrive.'

God is the Miner and Refiner of leaders. He wants to refine his leaders so that they bring fruitful offerings that are pleasing in his sight. The leaders he gives to us are precious and very valuable. We need to see them and treasure them accordingly. Jesus is ever calling and equipping leaders to join him in his kingdom work. Let's cooperate with him in that mining and refining process.

Tom Camacho

Part 1

GOD'S MINING PROCESS: DISCOVERING GOLD

1. EYES TO SEE

Seeing as God sees

In a small town far from the places of power and prestige, a story was unfolding that would change a life, transform a nation and alter the course of history. A group of brothers, a father and the national prophet were standing inside the home of a shepherd family near Bethlehem. At the request of the man of God, they were waiting for the youngest son, barely older than a boy, to come down from the hills where he was watching the family's flock of sheep.

Stick in his hand and a leather sling across his muscular shoulders, he was nothing special to look at . . . on the surface. Tanned from the sun, smelling of sheep and comfortable with the outdoors, he looked much like other boys in Israel; but this boy was different. God had a plan for this young shepherd. God was looking for a leader in the young David.

His brothers saw an annoying and precocious little brother. His father, Jesse, saw a faithful employee in the family shepherding business. The young man could only see he was a shepherd, a lowly vocation, and he was the youngest in his family. He often got left with the most menial jobs. He did know one thing, however: he was pretty skilled with rocks and a sling.

The boy could not see what his future held. His brothers definitely did not see much ahead for him. His father could not have seen much potential in him. If he had, he would have invited him to be present for the prophet's visit. The only one who saw the riches and potential inside David that day was God himself. God could see the precious gold in his servant David.

The prophet was on a king-seeking mission. The Spirit had told him to go to Jesse's house and anoint the next ruler of Israel. You see, Samuel was a man of God who had faithfully obeyed the voice of the Lord all his life. He had done God's bidding for decades. He knew how to hear from God, and his great passion was to obey the voice of the Lord. It is said of Samuel that 'none of his words fell to the ground'. That means he regularly heard from God and spoke God's words to the people. Samuel wanted what God wanted, but on this day, when it came to seeing kingly potential inside David, even the great Samuel missed it.

As the tall, handsome and confident Eliab appeared before him, Samuel said, 'Surely the Lord's anointed is before him.' He likely thought to himself, 'What a good-looking boy. He would make a great king.' Samuel saw Jesse's boys with human eyes, but God saw them differently. God was about to teach Samuel, and all of us, a huge lesson. He spoke to Samuel.

'Do not look at his appearance or at his physical stature, because I have refused him. For the Lord does not see as man sees; for man looks at the outward appearance, but the Lord looks at the heart.'

Humbled but expectant, Samuel kept waiting, while Jesse's family stood around pondering what on earth was going on.

Then it happened. David stepped into the house, and Samuel's eyes were opened. God showed the prophet who David really was. By the Spirit of God, Samuel saw the gold inside this young man: the heart of a warrior, the courage of a champion and the noble bearing of a king. Samuel saw that this was no ordinary boy, but Israel's future king, a national treasure, and a true 'man after [God's] own heart' (1 Samuel 13:14, NIV).

'Arise,' the Lord said to Samuel, 'anoint him. He is the one!'

'Then Samuel took the horn of oil and anointed him in the midst of his brothers. And the Spirit of the LORD rushed upon David from that day forward' (1 Samuel 16:13, ESV).

God used Samuel to see and draw out the gold he had placed inside David. Then he took David through a refining process to purify the gold inside him. It was a gruelling and painful process, but a necessary one. He does the same with us. He mines for the gold in us and then does the work of refining us for his glory.

David would go on to slay giants, unify a nation and write songs that would encourage millions. He was Israel's greatest king, and through his leadership, God would defeat all their enemies and bring peace to their nation. God saw a treasure in David and he sees the treasure in each one of us too.

Here is the lesson God wants to teach us through the story of David:

> In order to see the gold God has placed in a person, we need to see them with the eyes of the Spirit. To draw out someone's true potential, we need to cooperate with the Spirit of God.

God is looking for Samuels, leaders who will see the gold in people by the Spirit and draw out those riches for his purposes.

God is looking for leaders who will partner with him to see and shape the Davids of the future. Coaching Leadership is how we mine for gold in others and cooperate in God's refining process. In my work as a pastor, leader and coach, I have seen men and women come alive through the active process of Coaching Leadership. I believe that Coaching Leadership can transform leaders, churches, communities and even nations. Coaching Leadership is a concept whose time has come.

The people around us are like clay pots, being fashioned with care and purpose on God's potter's wheel. He is continuously moulding and shaping them. He is fashioning them into vessels he can use. In Coaching Leadership, we become like the fingers of God, in close contact with the lives of people as God shapes them for his purposes. God is doing the moulding and shaping but he is using us in his processes.

> Coaching leaders help others see themselves the way God sees them.

They encourage leaders to take the right next steps to cooperate with God's design and purpose for their lives. Coaching Leadership becomes an active, ongoing lifestyle of developing those around us.

To live a Coaching Leadership lifestyle, we must cultivate a new vision for leadership. I want to share with you some practical steps for how to see others with God's eyes, draw out the treasure inside them and help them take steps towards their God-ordained future. Coaching Leadership takes the mystery out of developing leaders and gives us practical ways to engage in helping leaders thrive.

As Christian leaders, we need to thrive ourselves. We can only take people where we have been, and we can only give them what we have received. As we come into thriving personally, we can then help others come into their own thriving through the process of Coaching Leadership. I recommend that you go through the Mining for Gold process yourself as the first step in your journey to helping others thrive. Get a coaching leader to help you come into thriving.

Today, you may feel stuck and frustrated. You may feel you are unable to accomplish all you dream about for your ministry, church or city. You may have lost hope that you will ever come into the fullness of what God created you for. You are not experiencing thriving. I completely get this. I've experienced every one of these feelings. It's painful when you can't see any gold in yourself, and it feels as though no-one else sees it either. You feel overlooked and forgotten.

When I felt like that at one point, God came and changed things for me. He used many different people and processes to show me my God-given identity and unique design. In particular, he used coaching to show me how to cooperate with his refining process in my life. The tool of coaching changed my life and it can change yours too!

We must get a new lens on leadership. We need to develop the skills of Coaching Leadership. As we become Samuels, asking God to show us the gold in others, we will discover more Davids, Esthers, Daniels and Pauls in our midst than we ever dreamed possible.

My leadership journey

For years I struggled with the pain and frustration of my inability to see. I saw myself through my own broken lenses. I carried a false identity, which didn't line up with God's Word and hindered my growth. I felt handcuffed to harmful mindsets and behaviours. With those broken lenses, I remained stuck and small. My false identity kept me from bearing more fruit. I didn't see myself as God saw me. My true identity was hidden from my view.

God used different leaders to help me see myself as he saw me. Slowly, I started to get a more realistic and accurate view of myself. I started to see my identity as a loved son of my heavenly Father. I began to get clarity about my strengths and weaknesses. I started to let go of false narratives that kept me struggling in broken patterns. I began to understand and accept that I am a treasured and beloved son who has something to contribute to the bigger picture. I began to get traction in my calling. Let me share my story.

I grew up in a typical American household, going to school, playing sports and having fun along the way. At age eighteen, my eyes were opened and I saw the emptiness and selfishness in my soul. I knew I needed something more. At a beach retreat at the end of my freshman year of college, I asked God to forgive me of my sin, and I trusted Christ, placing my life in his hands. That year I also made a radical decision to join the Army Reserve Officer Training Corps (ROTC) at my university. My aim was to become a helicopter pilot and commissioned officer. I had a mission and a goal.

From my youngest days, leadership felt very natural to me. I regularly stepped out to lead my peers in sports. I loved learning about leadership in school and on the athletic field. After getting my army commission as a Lieutenant, I went to flight school and became a military aviator. Flying helicopters and leading a platoon was like a dream come true for me. I loved being an aviation leader, and worked hard to grow in my leadership.

The military taught me thousands of leadership lessons such as:

- Leadership is a form of servanthood, where we put others before ourselves.
- Vision and clear communication are critical to great leadership.
- Trust and integrity are the foundations of great leadership.
- The leader's role is to inspire others to pursue a vision for a better future and to help them find their part in that bigger picture.

After my time in the army, I was hired by the General Electric Company as a human resource coordinator and leadership trainer. I was thrilled to be in a company that placed a high value on leadership and leadership training. My role was to help leaders grow and learn the skills of empowerment as we manufactured thousands of parts for commercial and military engines. In the demanding pressures of a world-class manufacturing plant, I learned many more leadership lessons.

In the business world I learned about accountability, teamwork and tackling immense projects. I learned about the diligent care of details as I worked with machine operators who cared deeply and personally about the quality of their work. I learned about creative and logical problem solving as I worked with intelligent and experienced engineers, solving incredibly challenging mechanical problems.

In time, I was asked to travel to different GE locations teaching leadership seminars across the company. In each workshop, I helped traditional supervisors learn a new empowered form of leadership. Businesses were learning to do more with fewer people at that time. My role was to help managers see the need to let go of control and trust their employees, so everyone could become more productive. Working for GE was a huge leadership school for me.

In 1996, my life took a major turn. While I worked at GE, I also served in my local church in various roles. I found the tasks of ministry leadership very comfortable and natural, which somewhat surprised me. I never had a goal to be a pastor. I led worship, facilitated small groups and led outreaches. It was thrilling to see God use my gifts through the ministry of the local church. I never thought of a formal church leadership role; I just enjoyed offering my leadership gifts to serve God's kingdom.

One day the pastor and elders of my church in Wilmington, North Carolina, asked to meet with me. They encouraged me to consider leaving the corporate world to answer the call of pastoral leadership on my life. I was surprised and challenged by their words. It was something I had not considered deeply.

I sought God in prayer for days. During a long walk alone with him, I asked the Lord what he wanted. I heard clearly, 'Do this, and never look back.' I said 'yes' to the call of God on my life, and left the corporate world, taking my first job as a staff pastor in my local church.

In the world of the church, I learned a whole new set of leadership lessons, such as:

- Leadership principles from the military and corporate worlds need to be adapted to the work of God's kingdom.
- Prayer is the real transforming force in ministry.
- God is more interested in my faith and trust in him than in my gifts or my competency.
- Resting in the Father's love and relying on the Holy Spirit's power can move mountains.
- Effective spiritual leadership takes both gentle compassion and tough love.
- Healthy boundaries create emotional safety, and help us last for the long haul in ministry.

Though I learned all these leadership lessons, I still found myself unable to come into a place of rest and confidence as a Christian leader. I had a ton of leadership experience, but things had not yet come together in my mind. I still felt foggy about who I was and what God wanted from me. Sometimes the things you need are right in front of you, but you cannot see them. All the pieces of my identity and calling were there, but I couldn't put them together on my own. I needed help.

Then I experienced Christ-centred coaching.

The incredible gift of coaching

So many things came together for me when I experienced the gift of great leadership coaching. Coaching opened my eyes and helped me step into the clarity and momentum God had for me.

My introduction to coaching came about when I was trained as a leadership coach for our church planting efforts in the Vineyard. I loved coaching from the very beginning. It felt like something I was born to do. I threw myself into the practice of coaching and, in time, became the coaching coordinator for our church planting efforts. I helped equip and develop coaches to serve our church planting leaders.

When I became the national coordinator for coaching church planters, I was offered excellent personal coaching for eighteen months from my mentor, Bob Logan. As I was coached, it was like a light switching on inside me. I could see certain things about myself and my work for the first time in my life. Coaching transformed the way I saw my gifts, my passions and my weaknesses. It was as if my life was a puzzle and coaching helped pull all the pieces together and put them in their proper place. Coaching helped me see who I was and get clarity about what God had created me to do. God used my coach to mine for the gold in me and help me cooperate with his refining process. I then began to experience a new joy in my relationship with God.

Before I experienced coaching, I felt God had a plan for me and wanted to use me, but I couldn't make sense of it. I doubted myself over and over again. Working out of my own strengths was wearing me out. I felt stuck, alone and frustrated. Then I tasted coaching and got some clarity about God's role and my role in bearing fruit. During that season, I found a river of grace that continues to move me forward to this day.

I am now a professional coach and deeply love everything about coaching. I have invested many hours into Mining for Gold in leaders. One of my greatest joys is connecting one to one with leaders, helping them discover the gold inside them. I believe in the power of effective, Christ-centred coaching. I love listening to the Holy Spirit as I work with leaders to discover what God is up to in their lives. As a coach, I have learned how things like identity, design and passion work together to form a sweet spot in a leader's life. I have enjoyed helping leaders steward their time for greater fruit and more momentum. I truly love coaching.

Coaching helped me come alive.

When God brought together the pieces of my life, I experienced an explosion of Christ's life bursting forth from within. Coaching helped me face the things I needed to face while a caring person walked by my side. It helped me find keys for doors that seemed locked before. As I gained new perspectives about myself and my work, I felt I had permission to be myself. I saw things more clearly and life felt different. With greater clarity, I no longer felt I was stumbling through life. I knew the issues I was facing. I started owning the bad fruit

I was experiencing and making the necessary changes to get different results. I began to know where God was leading me and to take the strategic next steps to get there.

All these changes happened as I began to see differently through my coaching experience. God was mining and refining the gold in me, and he wants to do the same for you. You are a treasure and very valuable in God's sight. You carry a treasure inside you and God wants to bring forth that treasure for his glory and the good of others.

Seeing what you have

In 1799, twelve-year-old Conrad Reed was walking through Little Meadow creek on his family farm in Cabarrus County, North Carolina. Wading through the shallow water with some friends, he was shooting fish with his bow and arrow. In the morning sunlight Conrad saw a bright substance flashing in the waters below him and stopped to investigate. Reaching down, he picked up a dense, 17-pound, shiny yellow rock that he thought was pretty neat.

Excited about his discovery, Conrad went home to tell his father, John Reed. John was a former Hessian soldier who had settled in NC after serving in the military. He bought land and dedicated himself to the disciplined life of farming. John was a practical, no-nonsense kind of guy.

'Daddy, look what I found,' Conrad said to his father. 'Isn't this a pretty yellow rock?'

'That's a nice rock, Conrad,' John said, largely disinterested in his son's discovery.

'What should I do with it?' the boy asked.

'Well, it's hot in here, son,' John said. 'Put it there on the porch to hold the door open, so we can get some breeze up here in the house.'

'Ok, Daddy,' Conrad said, and obeyed his father's request.

That 17-pound, shiny yellow rock remained a doorstop at the Reed home for nearly three years.

One day, in 1802, John got to thinking about that rock. He decided to take it to Charlotte to find out what it was. John showed it to a local jeweller, who immediately identified it as a chunk of solid gold. The jeweller didn't tell John the truth. Wryly, he asked John to name his price for the stone. John said, 'Three dollars fifty is fair,' and they agreed to the sale. John was pleased to get that amount for a rock. The sum of $3.50 was about a week's wages. John didn't realize that the gold nugget was actually worth $3600, a fortune at that time!

In the years following that discovery, the Reed family established a gold mine on their property. Many huge gold nuggets were discovered there in the coming years. The gold mine went on to make John Reed and his family very wealthy.

The lesson for us in this story of the Reed gold mine is this:

We need to see the value of the things (especially the people) that are right in front of us.

The greatest treasure is found in people, not shiny yellow rocks. The people around us are treasures of unimaginable worth. In God's eyes they are treasures of pure gold. When we cannot see through the eyes of the Spirit, we can't see the value they carry. People just look like average, ordinary rocks.

We can miss the value in the beautiful people around us every single day. We can treat people like doorstops, something of little value, when actually they are Davids in God's unfolding kingdom story. They could be instruments of God destined to transform a city or build up a nation. We need eyes to see their potential, and faith to believe God can use them mightily.

When we see people by the Spirit, the way God sees them, powerful things can happen. God can show us the gold inside people, and then teach us the skills to draw out that gold and help them cooperate with what he is doing. This is the heartbeat of Coaching Leadership. Mining for Gold begins when we start to see gold in the people around us.

Deeper-level questions

Great Coaching Leadership is marked by asking great questions. Great questions help us think more broadly and more clearly about what God is teaching us. Each chapter of this book contains thought-provoking questions to help you go deeper into the material.

1. When you look at the people around you, what do you see in them?
2. How would these people look to you if you saw them through the eyes of the Spirit?
3. What do you find most difficult about developing leaders?
4. How could you begin to cooperate with God to see the leaders around you through his eyes?
5. What would it look like to see leadership development through an abundance mentality?

Potential action steps

1. Pray and ask the Father how he sees the next person you meet.
2. Look for the gold, the Christ image, in each person you meet.
3. Ask the Father to show you the potential in every person by the Spirit.

2. COACHING: A FRESH LENS ON LEADERSHIP

Freeing people vs filling positions

I remember the moment it hit me.

Sitting in my first coaching workshop in Salt Lake City, Utah, I was excited to be trained and certified to coach leaders in our movement. I didn't exactly know what to expect, but I was ready to learn.

During a morning session, I listened to the presenters describe the power of coaching. They explained how coaching helps leaders find clarity for their lives and take helpful next steps. They taught us the value of the coaching relationship.

> The presenters showed us that the coach helps leaders get clarity on what work to do.

They spoke of the role of the Holy Spirit in developing a leader's potential. They told us that the leader does the work in the coaching process, not the coach. They taught us that the leader, not the coach, bears the responsibility for his or her own outcomes in the coaching relationship.

After watching several live coaching demonstrations, I began to see at first hand the power of effective coaching. I listened intently, growing more and more convinced that this coaching thing was a great fit for me and my passions. During one session the trainers got very specific on the power of clarity that coaching brings, and suddenly something exploded inside me. A revelation, like a bolt of lightning, shot through my being.

I could see in my mind how the tool of coaching, submitted to the Holy Spirit, could transform the way we practise leadership. Incorporating coaching principles into our daily practice of leadership would be powerful and transformative. The potential of that intersection lit up my spirit and flooded my brain. I could barely stay in my seat.

'We need to change the way we lead,' I thought to myself. 'Leaders need clarity to fulfil their calling. Coaching principles can take our leadership to a whole new level. We could learn to free people, not just fill positions.'

The concept of Coaching Leadership was released in my heart that day. I realized we needed to change our thinking about leadership and the way we train leaders. In that moment I sensed that if the coaching stream merged with the leadership stream, a river of blessing could be released to encourage many. I could see in my mind a generation of leaders helping other leaders, who helped other leaders in a multiplication flow. The potential was staggering. In that moment, it was as if thirty years of leadership experience and training collided with the powerful principles of coaching. The collision was electric in my brain.

Instead of building ministries by trying to fill positions, a coaching form of leadership would free people to become all

God had created them to be. Leaders would begin to discover who they were and how God had wired them. Then they could step into the roles and positions that made the most sense for their development and where they could bear the most fruit. By drawing out the gifts, callings and passions inside Christian leaders, those leaders could be deployed in the right roles where they could grow and flourish. It was a paradigm shift for me. I understood that coaching was more than a great tool to help leaders. The principles of coaching would give us a better way to lead.

The opportunity before us

Coaching Leadership has enormous potential. As coaching leaders we become developers of people instead of bosses who bark out orders telling everyone around them what to do next. We cooperate with the Holy Spirit as he develops the leaders in our midst. We learn to see the whole person we are developing and get the bigger picture of who that individual is and what he or she contributes. We look for people's unique, God-given passion and design, and help them find their sweet spot. We are not just interested in their skills and how they can help our organization accomplish its goals. We are interested in their well-being. It is a loving way to lead.

We think about how to help others flourish and look for roles that best suit their design. We encourage and empower them. We stop trying to get everyone to do what we want so this thing will grow. We live out a mentor/coaching style of leadership. It is a far better way to lead. We always remember a leader's growth is their responsibility. We remain open and available to them, but we are not driving their progress. We let them be responsible for who they are and where they are going.

Many of the leadership models of the past have placed the responsibility for development in the hands of the mentor or coach. In Coaching Leadership, we don't bear the weight of someone's growth. We simply draw out what's inside them. We don't own their outcomes, or manage their behaviour. We empower them. We give them permission to be themselves and use their gifts.

As we let go of the reins of managing people, we are freed up to pursue our own growth and development. Coaching Leadership lightens our load and reduces our stress. Empowering others brings health and balance to our role as leaders.

Coaching Leadership feels more like a shepherd leading sheep than a CEO building a corporation. It is much more relational, intimate and patient. The pace is slower and more relaxed. To become a coaching leader requires us to rest more in God's ability and cooperate more with his Spirit's work in people. I am convinced this is the way Jesus led his disciples and can be a fruitful way to practise leadership in any context and culture.

Ten benefits of Coaching Leadership

There are many benefits to Coaching Leadership, through practising an empowering leadership model. Let me share with you ten of the most significant.

1. *Less stress for you personally.* Empowering others through Coaching Leadership spreads the load of leadership across a capable team of leaders. When we learn to empower others we can actually experience a better quality of life! Our stress goes down when we let go of having to have all the answers and feeling that we are responsible for everything. We can focus on a narrower

scope: on those key things that we are best equipped to do for our team. Our leadership becomes like a powerful laser beam instead of a flickering candle.

Increased motivation and growth for your leaders. When leaders are being supported, heard and developed they get excited and are motivated to support your organization. Your load as their leader is reduced when leaders begin taking ownership of their own growth. Empowered leaders take responsibility for their own growth, determining their own next steps and pursuing their own future on their own terms.

2. *Multiplication of leaders.* When we learn to empower and develop leaders around us, we begin to have the leadership resources to respond to the growing challenges of our organization's growth. We all need more healthy, multiplying and empowered leaders. Having more leaders allows us to expand and do more of what we feel called to accomplish.

3. *Better relationships.* The skills of Coaching Leadership help our relationships go deeper. We listen better. We take the time to understand others. Deeper unity and understanding within your local team create a healthy, positive culture. Leaders are more open and transparent. Relationships get stronger.

4. *Better utilization of people's skills, gifts and resources.* Great stewardship is caring for the resources that belong to someone else. People, their talents and their skills belong to God. They belong to those people. When we are empowering we are developing the people around us so they can empower others – who can then empower others. We are bringing a return on the investment of resources God has placed in our care.

5. *More time for top leadership.* One of the sweetest fruits of the Coaching Leadership paradigm is the gift of time we receive from it. When we empower on a daily basis, we are freeing up time for ourselves to think more strategically, to consider the long-term implications and to hear the Holy Spirit. In Acts 6, when the church was growing and the apostles were being burdened by the increased load, they began to empower new leaders like Stephen and Philip. The empowerment of these leaders allowed the apostles to devote more time to their top priorities: prayer and the ministry of preaching and teaching God's Word.

6. *Greater creativity.* Creativity is a critical need in growing leaders. We need the freedom to think more broadly, try new things and dream what could be possible. When we empower others around us, as leaders we are free to dream, try new things and experiment. New things are happening all the time. It also opens up creativity in those you are empowering as they explore new possibilities for themselves. As empowerment increases, so does creativity. One opens up the fruit of the other.

7. *Better and faster responses to challenges and opportunities.* I love the concept of agile leadership. Great leadership teams respond to things coming at them with quickness, creativity and confidence. They are able to respond, not just react, because they have maximized the talents and strengths on their team. Empowerment cuts down bureaucracy and the requirement for checking in with the 'Boss'. Leaders on the team are empowered to make good decisions quickly to help the team achieve its goals. One last benefit is that problems are addressed in a timely and mature manner. Decisions happen more quickly and are more effective because leaders have

empowered others around them to help them think
things through clearly.

8. *More positive culture.* When we sow honour and
   value in every direction, we reap a more positive
   culture in our organization. People who have been
   loved and empowered are happier, more positive
   and more confident. When individual leaders are
   empowered, they meet challenges with more
   confidence. When more and more people are
   empowered, the atmosphere changes. The culture
   is more positive and the organization feels better
   about the future and where things are going. Love
   and respect are the foundations of empowerment, and
   empowerment is the foundation of a great corporate
   culture.

9. *Healthier families, churches and organizations.* The skills,
   attitudes and principles of empowerment are also great
   tools for being better husbands, wives, parents and
   family members. Listening, asking great questions and
   cooperating with the Holy Spirit are extremely helpful
   in raising kids and supporting our spouses. Healthy
   and wise boundaries create safety and the oxygen for
   everyone in the family to grow. When we empower
   those around us it's like a greenhouse: people are
   positioned to get established, grow deeper roots and
   flourish.

The challenge of leadership development

I have found that almost every leader asks these two questions
of God:

- Who have you created me to be?

- What have you created me to do to serve you and your kingdom?

These two questions are deep and resonate with the core of who we are. Developing leaders is deep work. There are no quick-fix answers to these core issues. I think there are two main reasons why leadership development is so challenging.

1. *Complexity.* The sheer complexity of bringing together all the pieces of one's identity, gifts, passions and experience in a clear and helpful way is daunting. We ask ourselves deep questions that have no easy answers: Who am I? What does God want of me? How does my experience intersect with my passions? How do I earn a living while devoting time to the deeper places within me? How do my gifts fit into the greater picture of what God is doing? What do I do when I have deep places of pain and brokenness inside me? These are all important to ask. We need a path and a process to help people answer these types of questions.

2. *Isolation.* Many leaders have no-one they can process their lives with. They don't have the help they need for breakthrough and growth so they remain stuck and frustrated. Their issues are causing all kinds of problems but they are not sure how to change them. They don't know where and with whom it is safe to share their deepest pain. Instead of learning and growing through God's refining processes, they just endure and survive to live another day. Their hearts are sinking and they are suffering alone.

This is where Coaching Leadership can make a huge impact. Coaching cuts through the complexity of our growth and helps us put the pieces together that lead to thriving. Just as Barnabas helped Paul get launched into his world-changing calling, coaching leaders help others find their calling and thrive.

Beginning from the wrong source

The number of self-help books in the world is incredible. The huge volume of them reveals something about us. We are all searching for more. We long to experience fullness in this life. We are hunting for the next five-step method to make all our dreams come true. We are searching out a clear and straight path into thriving, but it often eludes us.

We are looking for answers around our identity, design and calling. We long for a book or podcast from some guru to help us make sense of it all. But there's a problem. Most self-help materials begin from a wrong premise. They begin with self, with us. They explain ways we need to think differently or act differently to find sure success and fulfilment. They give us 'The five steps to thriving' or 'The four keys to lasting happiness' or 'The three lessons to live the life you've always dreamed'. But the source is wrong. We will never experience real and lasting thriving when we begin with ourselves. To thrive we must begin with God.

God created you. He is the great Gold Miner and Refiner. He loves you deeply and knows you personally. He made you and knows why you are here. He has the power and wisdom to bring you into the thriving you desire. He can make you come alive from the inside out. God has everything needed to bring forth the gold inside you.

The beauty of Coaching Leadership is that it cuts through the complexity of life and brings us to the clear, doable next steps for our future. Coaching takes what is complex and helps us see the simple next steps in our journey.

Here's a good definition of coaching from a great coach and leader:

> Coaching is the process of coming alongside a person or team to help them discover God's agenda for their life and ministry and then cooperating with the Holy Spirit to see that agenda become a reality.
> (Taken from a coach training session with material developed by Bob Logan)

Simplifying the process

Great coaching simplifies the complexity of leadership development. Coaching is one of the most effective leadership development tools we can use today. With coaching, we can simplify the leadership development process. We can break down thriving into its component parts. A coach is trained and skilled at helping bring simplicity out of complexity.

> Coaches become thinking partners who help leaders discover what is most important in their busy lives and move them towards a more fruitful future.

This list contains a few important things to consider about coaching and being coached as leaders:

1. *Coaching gives us the help we need tailored to our unique situation.* So much leadership development energy and so many resources are spent on off-the-shelf training and information that are helpful, but may not meet our particular needs. Coaching brings home ideas and lessons that are more specific to what we are seeing and experiencing in our daily lives.

2. *Coaching helps us discover how our unique gifts and experience add value in our context.* One of the greatest benefits of coaching is that it helps us bring together the various puzzle pieces of our lives and leadership. None of us are copies of other leaders. We are each one-of-a-kind treasures and to come into thriving we need to understand our unique identity, live from our unique design and do what we alone were created to do.

3. *Coaching helps us find momentum.* As leaders we can get stuck in ruts and patterns that keep us from moving forward. Coaching breaks the logjam of unhelpful thinking and behaviour, and gets the river of our leadership flowing again. It helps us move past our blind spots and see the way forward. Coaching pulls us out of our ruts. Staying stuck is a horrible place to be. Coaching helps us find momentum.

4. *Coaching helps us see the path ahead.* Coaches help us see the future in living colour. Through a process of discovery, coaches help us envision what can be and show us there is a way forward. Coaching is future focused.

5. *Coaching takes us from the big picture to the practical.* Coaching doesn't leave us up in the stratosphere, but helps us determine simple, doable next steps that lead us forward and release fresh momentum. The Spirit can do incredible things through simple acts of obedience.

6. *Christ-centred coaching welcomes the power of the Holy Spirit.* Godly coaching invites the power of the Holy Spirit to do the heavy lifting of leadership development. He is the Mining Engineer. He does the transforming. We just listen and discover what the Father is doing, and cooperate.

There is a rising generation of leaders who want more. They not only want to participate in the important things God is doing locally and around the world; they want to thrive in every dimension of their lives. They want healthy bodies, strong marriages and great families while they seek to thrive in their work. I think this is a very positive development. I dream of an army of coaching leaders dedicating themselves to raising up a new generation of thriving leaders. These leaders will shape the future and influence the leaders who will be shaping things well after we are gone.

Let's learn about Coaching Leadership from one of the great coaching leaders in the Bible.

A New Testament coaching leader

> And when Saul had come to Jerusalem, he tried to join the disciples; but they were all afraid of him, and did not believe that he was a disciple. But Barnabas took him and brought *him* to the apostles.
> (Acts 9:26–27, NKJV)

Nervous leaders were pacing the room, shaking their heads and wrestling with their thoughts. The discussion on the table was about the man Saul and what to do with him. Arguments had erupted around the discussion of his conversion and whether he had a future role in the work of the gospel. The disciples were trying to decide what to do. Things were not going well.

Everyone knew Saul's history. Many knew personally the people he had arrested, put in prison or had beaten. Some of those people had died. This man had caused immeasurable pain in Jerusalem and all across the nation. Now the disciples were expected to receive Saul as a disciple of Jesus and welcome him on to their ministry team as if he were one of their own. Impossible.

Similar to David's story, the only one to see the gold inside Saul at first was God himself. God needed a Samuel, a human instrument, to draw out that gold. First God came to Ananias, a godly, prophetic brother, and informed him that Saul was a man he had chosen and would use mightily. The Holy Spirit told Ananias he was shaping Saul into a powerful preacher, author and leader who would change the world. God asked Ananias to trust him; the gold was there. Ananias obeyed and prophesied to Saul about the gold inside him. This is what God told Ananias about Saul: 'Go, for he is a chosen vessel of Mine to bear My name before Gentiles, kings, and the children of Israel. For I will show him how many things he must suffer for My name's sake' (Acts 9:15–16, NKJV).

Despite God's endorsement of Saul, the disciples at Jerusalem were having none of it. It was too risky. They were not seeing Saul by the Spirit yet. Then one person changed his mind and endorsed him. This man's word and his example would alter the tide of public opinion around Saul. His endorsement of Saul would truly shake the world. Barnabas saw the gold in Saul.

Barnabas was a leader everyone respected. He was a godly, gracious and gentle father in the faith. His reputation was established through years of faithful service, solid teaching and generous giving. The early church leaders trusted him to go and help some of the very first churches as they were getting established. His integrity and his life of consistent faith were unquestioned. But now Barnabas was taking a huge risk. He was putting all that favour and trust on the line for one powerful reason: by the Spirit he saw something profound in the man Saul of Tarsus, later to become Paul. Despite the anxious caution in the leaders of the early church, Barnabas saw past Paul's broken history. He saw the gold in him and recommended him for leadership in the growing work of the gospel. Barnabas didn't see a liability in Paul; he saw an apostle.

Barnabas sensed the prophetic words were true: Paul was a chosen instrument of God. He sensed this intense man carried inside himself the mixture of character and gifts that was desperately needed for the advance of the gospel. Barnabas saw that Paul was not a threat; he knew he was a gift. He knew it by faith and by the Spirit.

The rest is history. Paul's life was like a torch God lit to spread the flame of the gospel all over the known world. His life and ministry have changed lives and cultures for centuries and they are still changing lives and transforming cultures to this day. Barnabas was a critical component in the release of Paul's powerful ministry. He saw the gold in Paul and drew it out.

For me, Barnabas is the perfect biblical picture of Coaching Leadership. His life and his relationship with Paul are a living picture of Mining for Gold. Barnabas was not afraid to let another leader outshine him. He was selfless and kingdom focused. His first concern was not the growth of his own ministry. He cared about the kingdom more than his own success or reputation. He saw Paul through the eyes of the Spirit and the lens of the kingdom. He sensed great treasure inside the man and drew out that potential. He helped Paul cooperate with his apostolic calling and begin to function in that call. We owe Barnabas much gratitude for his Coaching Leadership with Paul, the apostle.

Barnabas serves as a shining example of what God wants to do in our day. He cooperated with God, the great Refiner, in the development of the leader, Paul. Barnabas faced an incredibly complex leadership development situation and allowed the Holy Spirit to bring Paul into his world-changing calling. Let's follow in the footsteps of Barnabas, the radiant biblical model for Coaching Leadership. Let's cooperate with God as he brings forth leaders who will build his kingdom and make an impact on the world.

Deeper-level questions

1. What interests or excites you about the concept of Mining for Gold in others?
2. When you hear the word 'coaching', what immediately comes to your mind? Is it positive, negative or neutral? What is underneath those thoughts?
3. What is exciting about the possibility of helping many leaders thrive?
4. How would you describe your leadership development journey?
5. How could a coaching leader help you in your development?

Potential action steps

1. Look around you and ask the Father if there is someone he would have you invest in as a coaching leader.
2. Consider getting more training in coaching, or hosting a Coaching Leadership workshop in your local setting.

3. COMING ALIVE

> But he knows the way that I take; when he has
> tested me, I will come forth as gold.
>
> Job 23:10, NIV

Learning to thrive

I felt lost in the middle of my own life.

Like a ship tossed on a stormy ocean, I was adrift and my compass was broken. Pain and problems were coming at me like waves and threatening to swamp my boat. I was nowhere near thriving; I was hoping to survive.

Two years before, my wife Beth and I had stepped out to plant a new church in a bustling college town. For years we had dreamed of planting a new church and seeing countless lives touched and transformed by the Lord. We took a step of faith and gathered a small team to help us see the vision fulfilled.

We began full of hope and enthusiasm as our team bought houses, made friends and prayed for God to build his kingdom through us. It felt so exciting as, together, we pursued a greater purpose and a future full of possibilities. We did life together, experienced God's grace and saw a small community start to form.

Life was good . . . for a season.

Then something shifted. Like a slow leak in an otherwise perfectly good tyre, it felt as though something was not right. We didn't know exactly what it was, and certainly had no idea how bad it was. For a season we carried on hoping that things would get better. They didn't.

Slowly, the church plant started to unravel. It wasn't pretty. Problems I had not addressed out of fear and insecurity came back with a vengeance. Relationships were fraying and issues were coming to the surface that I didn't know how to handle or process in a healthy way.

Most disturbing, I began to see the gaps in my own leadership. I'm sure others saw my broken places, but I was blind to them. I had worked for years trying to become an effective leader, but there were things I still didn't understand and hadn't addressed inside me. The reality of the abundant life was a foreign concept to me. My weak relationship with the Father resulted in a leadership style that looked a lot like striving, and nothing like abiding.

I had never learned my true identity in Christ. I lived by leadership techniques or the latest new book, fad or idea I'd got from my last leadership conference. All the while, my inner world remained immature and undeveloped. Fear and insecurity were now manifesting outwardly in my relationships and my decisions. It was difficult to face how shallow and immature I truly was. Letting go of my control scared me to death, but I sensed God wanted to heal me and set me free more than he wanted me to feel good in the short term. He wanted to give me the life he'd created me for.

You can only give what you have and you can only lead others where you have been. Because I had never come fully alive in Christ myself, I had no framework or understanding to help others come alive. I had no rest in my identity, no clear direction and no defined purpose.

Things went from bad to worse and a severe mercy landed in my life. What, months ago, had felt like an exciting dream now felt like a tragic nightmare. The church plant was falling apart, and people were leaving in droves. Some leaders were very angry with me. My desperate attempts to hold the church together were failing.

When it was clear the church would not survive, we told everyone it was over and held a memorial service to honour all those who had given and served to help make that church possible. It felt as if something inside me died that day. My hopes seemed like a sunset fading into darkness.

The hardest part was looking at the specific issues in me that led to the church collapse. I had to face my sin and my broken inner world. When you've never faced your shadow, it's like a door you don't want to open for fear of what you'll find inside. You know there's something in there, but it seems easier to ignore it. Unfortunately, ignoring it only prolongs the pain.

Despite my fears and pain, I couldn't ignore the issues any longer. I had no choice. God was breaking down my doors of fear and insecurity because he loved me and wanted to set me free. He wanted to show me what he'd created me for. He wanted a son who would come home and live fully alive. He wanted to place my feet on something solid and fill me with his life.

Sometimes God's love goes beyond our fears and our resistance to get to the root of the problem. His love is at times severe and relentless. We may not understand what he is doing at every step of the process, but God always comes with the desire to give us life. His ways are sometimes hard to grasp, but his heart for us is always good. God broke me so he could set me free. He broke down my doors of fear and brought me out of bondage so he could bring me into his life.

The gift of caring leaders

When the church closed, I found a job teaching at the local high school. I honestly felt that God could never use me for much of anything. I felt I was too broken for him to use. I could only see my mistakes and the pain I had caused others. Thankfully, God saw more in me than I could see in myself. He saw gold somewhere in my broken pile of dirt and debris.

As I tried to make sense of the pain, God sent caring leaders into my life to listen to me, pray for me and help me process my pain. God knew that I needed to grow significantly on the inside for what was ahead of me. He knew I needed a stronger and healthier inner world to steward a growing ministry. Step by step, with the help of caring leaders, God dismantled my broken identity and started to show me what he saw and desired for my life. These caring and compassionate leaders helped me sift through the broken and scattered pieces of my life and find the gold that was still there. I began to sense that God was not done with me yet. They showed me there was still hope for me. I started to come up out of the pit of my pain.

This is the gift of having coaching leaders in our lives. With their help, we begin to depart from our patterns that have kept us small and bound up. We face our issues. We start to process life on a deeper level and find answers to questions we have been asking for years.

> Coaching leaders don't just look at our symptoms.
> They get to the core issues that need a touch from God.

Things were getting clearer. I experienced the first trickle of what thriving felt like. I was coming alive.

Grace to be

Becoming a godly, thriving leader does not happen apart from God's work of grace in the human heart. For years I had a fuzzy picture of God's grace. I knew grace as favour I didn't deserve. I understood that concept in my head, but grace is so much more. Grace is also God's unlimited power available to us for everyday living. Grace allows us to rest and lie back into God's love. When we understand grace, it's like placing a plant in the sun. The light and warmth of God's grace transforms us at a cellular level and changes the way we see God, his Word and our mistakes.

As I began to understand more clearly God's unfailing grace, my inner world started to slow down. In grace, I could rest in his presence. Grace helped me let go of endless analysing and rethinking the details of my life. Grace gave me an upgrade to a new operating system. When I faced certain challenges, I worried less and began to trust. I drew closer to God and allowed his love and power to steady me and bring me forward. Life began to come together in a holistic way, and I started to taste the first fruits of thriving.

The revelation of God's grace brings power and strength in lots of specific ways. Grace helps us let go of judging every detail of our lives and the lives of others. Grace helps us allow others to live their own lives. We stop judging others' choices. Grace slowly quiets our anxiety and endless striving. We stop trying to fix ourselves and we trust in his grace to bring us into his promises. By the Holy Spirit, grace becomes an inner spring of living water, a fountain we can turn to at any moment in any situation to find strength, peace, love and healing. Grace gives us the courage to look under the hood of our life and leadership. With the help of coaching leaders in our lives, we actually make progress towards maturity.

God's grace gave me the courage to face the reality of all that had happened with the failed church plant; the courage to own the bad choices I had made. I went to people I had hurt and asked for their forgiveness. God's grace broke me of my need to be right and in control. It helped me turn from my selfishness and begin to seek how I could become a source of love and encouragement to others. Clarity about God's grace helped me encounter the good news of the gospel and that gospel is transforming me daily. I have tasted the sweet, living water of grace.

The gift of clarity

As I worked with the coaching leaders God sent into my life, I discovered an incredible, life-changing truth:

> Coaching Leadership helps us find clarity. Clarity leads
> to momentum and a true experience of thriving.

One of the greatest obstacles to thriving is our ongoing lack of clarity. We have blind spots and so we can't see the real issues affecting us. Since we can't define the real problems, we don't know how to solve them.

When we lack clarity about who God is, we often feel very alone. Not knowing his fatherly care makes us feel like orphans, living scared on the streets of a big city. We don't feel we have a home. We may have an advanced degree with tons of knowledge about God, but still not know him as a loving and present Dad who believes in us. The reality of God's nature is not clear to us.

When we begin to see him distinctly as a faithful, loving Father, everything inside us starts to change. We find we are not alone, we have more hope and we don't fear the future. When we clearly see the gracious heart of our Father, we can come home from the pigsty and find we belong in his family (Luke 15). With clarity about God's heart towards us, we learn we are not only forgiven, we are favoured, blessed, provided for and celebrated. Getting clarity is like a prodigal coming home. No more living with the pigs.

We can also lack clarity about ourselves. Without a clear picture of how a loved son or daughter lives, we struggle to receive God's blessings and favour. We try to fix all our problems and often make them worse. We are busy doing lots of stuff, but have no sense of a larger story and how we fit into it.

> Clarity changes everything. With clarity we can see the larger story. When we get clarity around our Christ-centred identity, thriving is the natural result.

Clarity brings momentum to our efforts. With clarity, we come alive in his love and that love begins to flow through us. We are moving from existing to thriving.

Clarity is the key

Here are some areas where we need clarity:

- the goodness of God
- our identity as his loved sons and daughters
- our design
- our motives
- our passions
- our pain
- our time.

Clarity leads to momentum. Biblical thriving is about coming into the fullness of all God has for you.

Let's go deeper into each of these areas where we need clarity.

The goodness of God

Getting a clear picture of God's goodness is the foundation of thriving. Everything begins with our view of God. When we know who he is, it shapes everything else. If we see him as gracious, merciful, compassionate and patient, we will relate to him that way. When we see clearly all he's done to rescue us from our selfishness and sin, everything shifts.

Carrying a false view of God means our behaviour reflects that false view. If we think he is angry and judging us every moment, our hearts respond accordingly. We run from him and hide. The image of God you carry inside your mind and heart is one of the most critical parts of who you are. If you have a wrong view of him, you cannot really know who you are.

When we see God's love clearly, something settles inside us. Love becomes a solid foundation under our feet. It never moves. We can build on it. Clarity in our view of God is the foundation, but there's more.

Our identity

Before my ministry crash, I had no clarity in my identity. I was consumed with focusing on what was wrong in my life. I was problem focused. I was task driven. I wore myself out thinking about what was wrong with me and about the things I wasn't doing right.

When we get clarity that we are treasured sons and daughters of God, we experience incredible peace and rest. In 2 Corinthians 5:17, Paul writes: 'if anyone is in Christ, he is a new creation. The old has passed away; behold, the new has come' (ESV)

When we get clarity in our identity, we discover we are new creations, no longer ruled by sin. We find that something incredible has happened to us. We are no longer slaves, aliens or orphans. We are treasured members of God's family and begin to experience deep and lasting freedom.

We learn that God has placed his righteous nature inside us, and now we are right with him because of what Jesus has done for us. We discover we are not on the outside, rejected by God. We are loved sons and daughters with an inheritance of riches from our Father.

We can then stop focusing on all our problems and focus instead on all the promises God has given us in his Word. We start feeling at home in our own skin. We move beyond survival and focus on stewarding all the blessings God has given us. The greatest fruit of clarity in our identity is a deep and lasting inner rest. From that rest we find we have more energy for what God is calling us to do.

Our design

For years I lacked clarity in my design. I never took the time to discover how I was uniquely fashioned and wired. I tried to be like everyone I read about or listened to. That process left me tired, discouraged and frustrated.

When I got clarity in my design, I realized that I am created and gifted to do certain things well. There are a few things that I do quite naturally. They don't feel like work to me but like a normal part of who I am. When I do them it feels as if I'm doing what I was born to do. When I live in the clarity of my unique design, life has a natural flow.

God calls us his masterpiece. Ephesians 2:10 says, 'For we are His workmanship, created in Christ Jesus for good works, which God prepared beforehand that we should walk in them' (NKJV).

We are a one-of-a-kind work of art. As David said in Psalm 139, we discover we are beautifully and wonderfully made. God's divine fingerprints are all over our lives. Clarity of design gives us permission to be ourselves and leads to a wonderful momentum in our walk with him.

When we lack clarity in our design, we waste time and energy doing things we don't enjoy. We all have to do things we don't enjoy, but what if we were able to spend most of our time doing the things we do enjoy and the things we are naturally good at? What a life that would be. More on this later.

Our motives

Before my ministry crash, my motives for ministry were rooted in selfishness and striving. Since I had no sense of identity as a person, my efforts came from a deep place of fear. I felt I was a nobody and I had to do something important to become a somebody.

I was performing so I could be loved and accepted. Performing became the main motive for my life. From an empty cup, I burned myself out trying to give others water I didn't have. It was exhausting. I couldn't do ministry that way any longer.

When we face the selfish desires underneath our motives, we must repent. Through God's forgiveness and restoration, our motives begin to change. We want to bless others in the way we have been blessed by God. We want to help them find the love and grace we have experienced. We want to steward our gifts, time and abilities to help others. We no longer need to prove we are valuable. We offer our gifts and our time to God and ask him to use them for his purposes.

Our passions

For years I lacked clarity around my own passions. It felt
as though I was always living someone else's life. I had no
centre and no source, and it showed. When I took the time
to identify and write down the issues I was most passionate
about, it was like a light bulb coming on inside me. I began to
sense that those passions weren't just coming from myself.
They were God's passions coming through my personality.

When we get clarity around our passions, we give ourselves
permission to focus on them. We begin to discover how our
design can be uniquely used by God to pursue those passions
and bring real change. We experience more alignment, which
leads to greater momentum. We start feeling a synergy that
is deeply satisfying and truly exciting. I can feel it right now,
writing these words.

Our pain

I don't like pain. For years I avoided it whenever I could. I
became an expert in denial. As a result, I remained stuck,
chained to patterns that were toxic. It was sad and frustrating.

Now I see pain more clearly. Pain is not the enemy. False
beliefs are the enemy. Lies are the enemy. We can waste years
running from pain and avoiding difficult truths about
ourselves. But when we get clarity around our pain, we can
pursue the healing we need. We can stop fearing pain and
begin to embrace it. Pain helps us see where something is
unhealthy inside us. When you find out what's causing the
pain, you can get the help you need.

Pain can save our lives, but without clarity, it is like being sick
and not knowing what's wrong. You feel awful but you don't
know what's causing it. You can lose hope of ever being whole.

Clarity in our pain can bring us into the truth that sets us
free. When we surrender to the pain of God's healing process,

the sun of his love begins to rise in our hearts. We feel its warmth and life. God begins to reassemble our broken pieces. Pain helps us get the healing we need to thrive.

Our time

In my early life, time was an elusive mystery I could never master. I lived a reactionary life ruled by the scream of urgent things. Because I had no clarity around my time, I never got to important matters.

When we get clarity around our identity and our design, time starts to make sense. We know who we are and what we do best, so we begin to know what to do with our time. Time becomes a rich resource we want to wisely invest into our passions and our purpose.

When clarity comes around time, we feel like a bird set free from a cage. We slow down inside and begin to examine where our time is going, and how we are spending it. We move from spending time to investing it. Time becomes our friend. We learn how to align our time and efforts with our passions and our design. The result is even more momentum. It's incredible.

Clarity leads to momentum

As coaching leaders, we want to help leaders find the clarity they lack. When things are unclear, we don't know the way forward, we waffle between options and our momentum slows down. In Coaching Leadership, we come alongside leaders and help them get crystal clear on what they are feeling, where they are struggling and what they feel God is calling them to do. This clarity helps them make concrete next steps that lead them forward. Those small steps lead to small wins, and a string of small wins leads to momentum.

Leaders need others to help them come into thriving. Choosing to live a Coaching Leadership lifestyle positions you to be a resource for leaders around you. Help those around you get clarity and get those wins. Help them find some momentum. Help them discover the gold they carry and invest it in the kingdom in a positive way.

Deeper-level questions

1. What makes clarity so powerful for us as leaders?
2. Where do you lack clarity right now in your life or leadership?
3. Why does clarity lead to momentum?
4. In the difficult, painful parts of your journey, how could a coaching leader have been a help and a resource for you? How could that help have had an impact on you?
5. What did God teach you as you walked through your most difficult moments?

Potential action steps

1. Write down three or four areas in your life where you lack clarity.
2. Pray and ask God to give you his heart and perspective for you in those areas.
3. Who could you ask to come alongside you in your leadership development journey?

4. MINING FOR GOLD

> Now when the turn came for Esther the daughter
> of Abihail the uncle of Mordecai, who had taken
> her as his daughter, to go in to the king, she
> requested nothing but what Hegai the king's
> eunuch, the custodian of the women, advised.
> And Esther obtained favor in the sight
> of all who saw her.
>
> Esther 2:15, NKJV

A gold discovery

In her young life, Esther had already experienced so much pain and loss. After her parents' tragic death, Mordecai, her older cousin, took her in as his own daughter. Under his loving care, Esther began to heal and mature into a young woman of purity and character. Neither she nor Mordecai could imagine what would unfold for her over the next few months.

Esther was especially lovely. Everyone who met her could see that, but her beauty went deeper than her looks. There was gold inside this young woman, a strength and devotion that God would use to preserve his chosen nation. God saw what was inside Esther. Soon, the whole nation would see it too.

Mordecai saw a young girl who would make someone a wonderful wife one day. Maybe she would marry a butcher or a baker or, with great fortune, a noble businessman or government official. Like Samuel with David, Mordecai saw Esther through natural eyes, but God saw her through the Spirit. God knew what was ahead for her, and he was preparing her to be his instrument. He saw inside her the courage and character that would be needed for her particular assignment. God saw the gold within.

When the knock came at the door and the court official announced that all eligible young women would be evaluated as potential wives for mighty King Xerxes, Mordecai worried for Esther. She was young and innocent. She could be eaten alive in the beauty pageant atmosphere of the king's wife-choosing process. She was inexperienced in the ways of the world and the dynamics of palace life.

'Don't tell them you are a Hebrew,' he told her, 'but don't forget you are one either.'

Once inside the queen-selection process, Esther caught the eye of the chief eunuch, Hegai. This important government leader was in charge of the young maidens and their beauty treatments as they prepared for their encounter with the king. Hegai noticed something different about Esther. He could see something deeper and more attractive in this young woman that went beyond her physical features.

He thought to himself, 'She's beautiful, but a lot of these girls are naturally attractive. There is something special about this girl. I can't yet identify exactly what it is.'

Hegai took a special interest in Esther. God gave her favour with him and he began to coach and mentor her for her coming night with the king. He told her what the king was like and what he preferred. Hegai could see that the purity and moral courage in Esther would be a gift to King Xerxes and a treasure for the nation as well. Secretly he hoped she would be selected.

When Xerxes met Esther, his heart was captivated by her. Her natural beauty drew him close, but her character and insight set her apart. He saw the gold in her. He joyfully selected her to be his wife and to rule with him as queen.

In time, Haman, one of the king's chief advisors, launched a plot to kill the Jews and plunder all their resources. Esther found herself in a position to be a change agent and be used by God to save Israel. The situation called for her to tap into the gold inside her and risk her life to save her people. She obeyed, and the Jews were saved.

Esther's story shows us how coaching leaders help us navigate difficult and frightening circumstances. We all, like Esther, need the help of others like Mordecai and Hegai, who see the gold in us and help to draw it out. We need people who will speak truth to us and encourage us to become all God created us to be.

Esther was born with natural beauty, but she lacked many things. She wasn't worldly wise or educated in the great schools of learning. She had no background to deal with the manipulation and cunning schemes of government workers. She had God's Spirit with her, but she needed others to draw out the treasure in her as God prepared her for her great assignment.

Mordecai and Hegai were Esther's coaching leaders. They played different roles in her life, but they were both used by God in her maturing process. They drew out of Esther things she could not see in herself. God created her and placed the treasure inside her, but he used these men to bring that gold to the surface. When God has a key, life-or-death assignment for someone, he takes the time to prepare them well, and he uses leaders and mentors to shape them for it.

The Mining for Gold process

In the early days of mining, gold miners would pan for gold. Panning was a process where they used running water to sift through rock, sand and dirt to find the valuable gold hidden in all that debris. As they panned along a creek or riverbed, the lightest substances like sand and small rocks would quickly run out of the pan. The heavier materials, the gold or diamonds, would remain in the bottom of the pan, ready to be discovered.

It is the same for us as coaching leaders. There are lighter, less important issues and tasks that our leaders are facing. Many leaders wear themselves out focusing on these lighter, lesser things. God wants them to focus on the heavier, more critical issues that will shape them for greater things. As coaching leaders, our role is to help them focus on the weightier issues of their lives: their identity, their calling, their character and their design. It's our job to help them distinguish between the light issues and the heavier ones. As we help them wrestle with the heavier issues, the Holy Spirit matures them, bringing them into greater freedom, insight and momentum on their journey. In Coaching Leadership, we don't make gold, but we walk with leaders as they discover the gold God put within them.

Gold mining in leaders is God's process. We don't have to create things or make things happen. The gold is in there. God put it there. Our task and privilege is to help leaders discover the gold they carry, understand it, and then take the next right steps to invest in kingdom purposes.

There are four primary parts to Coaching Leadership. I call it the **Mining for Gold process**. They are:

1. deep listening;
2. asking great questions;

3. cooperating with the Holy Spirit;
4. determining the right next steps.

I have worked with hundreds of leaders using this simple format. It's a simple but powerful process that leads to breakthrough results. As we learn to cooperate with the Holy Spirit, he can take these simple steps and unlock a leader's future. Like panning for gold, Coaching Leadership helps us find the gold inside every leader.

Don't be fooled by the simplicity of the model. The parts of the process work together synergistically and effectively to help leaders grow and mature. It is easy to overcomplicate things and overthink leadership development. Resist that tendency. Stay in your lane. Your role is to help a leader discover what God is doing in them and help them cooperate with it. You are helping them line up with what the Father is doing and drawing out the gold in them. Mining for Gold is simple and powerful.

Let's take a deeper look at each part of this process to see how the pieces work together to bring forth the gold in leaders.

Deep listening

Everything begins with effective, deep listening. One of the great gifts we can give people is quiet, uninterrupted space to share their thoughts. So many leaders feel isolated, lonely and overlooked. To deeply listen to them is an incredible gift and expresses great love and value to them. I have found deep listening gives life and oxygen to leaders. In our digital, high-speed world, deep listening is a rare and beautiful thing. It is profound in these fast-paced days to actually slow down and have a deep and meaningful conversation.

This is the gift we can offer others as coaching leaders. We offer them our full and focused attention to help them get clarity and momentum for their life and leadership. What makes Mining for Gold so powerful is the fact that most leaders rarely get the chance just to talk and process life with a caring, trusted friend. Deep listening is where this begins.

The Mining for Gold process begins with prayer. Before every Coaching Leadership session, I like to take a few minutes to thank God for the person and ask for the Holy Spirit to guide our conversation. I ask the Lord to make our session the most helpful it can be for the leader, and to show us what he is doing and how we can cooperate with his mining and refining process. When we invite the Holy Spirit into the coaching process, everything goes to a higher level.

Deep listening is the first step because it keeps God in charge of the process. One of the dangers of leadership development is to tell young leaders all the nuggets of wisdom we have acquired on our leadership journey. We become dispensers of leadership wisdom. But that puts us in the spotlight. The goal of the Mining for Gold process is to keep the spotlight on the leader we are working with. I have found that one nugget of wisdom a leader gets from God is worth ten thousand words of wisdom from me.

Prayer and deep listening help us clear our mind of our own thoughts, our own judgments and our own perceptions. Through deep listening, we let the person we are coaching share what they are thinking and feeling about their issue or situation. We don't talk. We let them talk. We keep the space open because listening is holy ground where true discovery and learning begin. We want to tread lightly in leaders' lives and be respectful and trustworthy as we listen and process their issues with them.

In the deep listening phase, we are not trying to get to any particular place in the conversation. People love to share freely about the important issues they are facing. In this first phase we are exploring, examining and deepening our understanding of what is really going on in the leader's life.

Early in the deep listening phase, I often ask leaders what they can celebrate about their current situation. This starts the coaching conversation on a positive note and encourages them to remember that God is already at work in their lives and some good things are happening. It also releases faith that God can work again today in their situation.

Deep listening helps us take the time to connect as friends before diving into deep and complex issues. It establishes trust for leaders that this process is about them and not us. Upon that foundation of trust, real and meaningful conversation can take place. God can take the conversation in powerful and transforming directions. If we dive too deeply into problems without getting to know the person, the tone of the conversation can remain tense and tight. Trust helps us move from the lighter issues to the heavier ones. When we listen deeply, trust opens up in our conversation and allows us to explore new possibilities and solutions.

Deep listening requires that we slow down and stop talking. In a great Coaching Leadership session, I try to let the leader talk at least 80% of the time. The coaching session is for them, not for me. I keep myself in check and quiet. Deep listening is a critical skill to the Mining for Gold process and where it all begins. Keep the conversation about them, not you. The goal is to help them get clarity and momentum for their lives and their issues.

A great reminder to keep ourselves in the right frame of mind is the acrostic WAIT: **W**hy **A**m **I** **T**alking? When we find we are doing most of the talking, it's time to pull back and re-engage our listening skills.

In deep listening, we are not trying to solve anything yet. We are determining with the leader what exactly the issue is they are facing and how they are feeling about it. We are assessing the depth of commitment they have towards solving the issue. We are also assessing the level of clarity they have about what they are facing.

The Coaching Leadership process is a 'come alongside' function. Like Barnabas in the Bible, our role is to walk beside the leader we are helping. So, just as Barnabas came alongside Paul, we come alongside leaders and help them become the leaders God created them to be.

> In Coaching Leadership, we don't solve leaders' issues for them or tell them what they need to do next.

If we do our part well, leaders feel they are in charge and they choose the path that is best for them.

With the trust and accountability of someone walking beside them, they are more likely to step out and try a few practical action steps that move them forward. Those action steps are simple but critical in their growth and momentum. We are merely thinking partners, accountability partners and facilitators of the person's growth.

Deep listening has become an absolute delight for me. I get so much joy from hearing the deeper parts of a leader's story and motivations. Processing the personal, core details of a leader's life is a huge privilege and a place of great trust. The things leaders share with us in our private sessions always remain strictly confidential.

As we listen to someone else, it is useful to invite the person to go deeper on any point that we feel is interesting and potentially helpful. We can invite him or her to say more by using phrases like, 'Tell me more about that', or 'Unpack that a little more for me'. Our goal in deep listening is to assist leaders to think about their lives and situations in a more helpful way than they were doing before.

In deep listening, we allow the conversation to go wherever the leader and the Holy Spirit want to take it. We approach the conversation with an open hand and an open heart, seeking clarity, which leads to growth and momentum. We are on a discovery mission trying to discern where leaders are, what they are facing and what God might be doing in their lives.

This is holy ground. Tread lightly, but dig deep.

Asking great questions

The primary tool of the Mining for Gold process is the skill of asking great questions. Insightful and penetrating questions are the power tools of Coaching Leadership. When we learn to ask tremendous questions, a whole new world of growth and discovery comes alive for us and the leaders we are working with.

Great questions are the key. Just one can unlock potential in a leader and launch him or her in a whole new direction.

There are great questions, OK questions and terrible questions. Let's look at a few characteristics of great questions.

Great questions are:

- open-ended, not closed-ended;
- designed to explore a topic more deeply, not gain information;
- deeper than what's on the surface;
- stimulating to encourage leaders to think more broadly about what they are experiencing;
- catalytic to help leaders further examine the underlying details and realities of their situation;
- completely about the leader, not about you.

One great question can change someone's life. Jesus used this skill repeatedly as he discipled his band of twelve leaders.

'Who do men say that I am?' he once asked them. After their response he dug deeper. 'And who do you say that I am?' He got more personal, taking the conversation from the broad to the specific. His open-ended questions had the disciples looking more deeply at their own thoughts and motives. This is what great questions do.

When we ask closed-ended questions (questions which require only a yes or no answer), we close down the conversation instead of opening it up. Closed-ended questions stop the discovery process and just give us surface information about what's going on. Avoid this type of question at all costs in an empowering leadership session. If you ask a closed-ended question and catch yourself, just stop and rephrase it in an open-ended format.

Great questions open up the conversation to entirely new directions and thought processes. Our aim is to help leaders think through their situation so they can take responsibility for their own growth. Through questions we encourage them to choose some next steps that assist them to move forward in a positive, new direction.

These few sample questions really help move things forward in an empowering conversation:

- What is the most challenging part of this situation for you?
- What are some other ways you could approach this situation?
- What would you really like to see happen?
- What are you afraid of?
- What gives you energy?
- What about this drains you? Or frustrates you?

- What will change for you if this goes the way you want?
- What is the most important aspect of this change for you personally?
- On a scale of 1 to 10, how motivated are you to accomplish this change?
- Where would you like to be in this area in five years?
- What are you most passionate about in this process?
- What is the Holy Spirit inviting you into in this?
- Where do you see the hand of God moving in this process?
- How is God changing you through this?

One key way to go deeper around an issue is to encourage the person by saying, 'Help me understand what you mean there.' Your goal is to find the gold and see where the Father is working in his or her life. There are an unlimited number of great questions. With practice and the help of the Holy Spirit, you can begin to ask the powerful questions that help others see their way through their problems and find strategies that lead to momentum and thriving.

Cooperating with the Holy Spirit

I find this third step the most exciting part about the Coaching Leadership approach. There are lots of leadership tools and strategies in the world, but there is nothing and no-one that can compare to the person and work of the Holy Spirit. The Holy Spirit is the catalyst that brings real power to the Coaching Leadership process.

Learning to cooperate with the Holy Spirit in a Coaching Leadership conversation is both exciting and transforming. I always begin my coaching times with prayer. I ask God to show us what he is doing in the life of the leader I am working with. I ask that he would make things clear and bring about the changes that will help that person thrive.

We practise dual listening. In dual listening, we are listening to the person while simultaneously listening to the voice of the Holy Spirit. It sounds complicated but God can teach you how to do it. God can show you what he is doing while you listen deeply to a leader in front of you. When God speaks, it changes everything. It is so exciting to hear and discern what the Father is saying over one of his kids!

God says in the Word about us: 'For I know the plans I have for you . . . plans to prosper you and not to harm you, plans to give you hope and a future' (Jeremiah 29:11, NIV).

We can be confident God is always doing something good and loving in a person's life, even in the midst of great pain. He is always working. Our job is to listen, watch and discern what it is he is doing and saying. If you ask the Holy Spirit to show you, he will!

Here are some indicators to see where the Spirit might be working in people's lives:

- *Strong emotions.* Sadness, grief, pain or frustration.
- *Anger.* Is there an area of deep hurt that needs healing? Some deep calling or work of justice coming?
- *Passion.* They light up whenever they talk about a particular scripture, ministry or issue. This is a key indicator of where God wants to move in their lives – a particular passion for a kingdom cause.
- *Fear.* God wants to help them move past their fears. Love drives out fear.
- *Excitement and joy.* What gets their hearts pumping faster and gives them hope for the future?
- *New discoveries or revelation.* Are they seeing things in ways they have never seen them before?

- *Simplification.* Sometimes the problem feels too complex. When God makes it simple, it empowers people to take the right next steps.
- *Clarity.* Seeing connections in the whole situation they have never seen before. Getting a clear perspective on the problem is very empowering.
- *Increased freedom.* God is setting them free to be who he created them to be.
- *Permission.* Feeling the freedom to be themselves and let go of unhelpful thought patterns.

Whenever you see these things happening in a leader's heart, they are like signal lights telling you God is at work. Using the tools of great questions and continuously listening for the work of the Spirit, you can help people make incredible strides in their growth and confidence. Watch for emotions, frustrations, pain and discouragement. Where you see these things, God is very near. When you walk closely with people and process the raw emotions they are feeling, you are near to the deepest part of their hearts and to the heart of God for them.

Trust the Holy Spirit, lean into him and watch for where he is working. The Spirit will show you where the Father is at work. Our role as coaching leaders is to join in where we see the Father working in a leader's life.

Determining the right next steps

The first three tools in the Mining for Gold process – deep listening, asking great questions and cooperating with the Holy Spirit – help bring the clarity and insight needed for positive change.

However, we must always keep in mind the purpose of our coaching session: helping leaders cooperate with God's Spirit, find momentum in their journey and step into the fullness of all God has for them. So, if we don't come away with action steps, we are not serving the leader in the best way we can. I always encourage one to three clear action steps in every empowering conversation.

As I am coaching leaders, I watch the time and make sure we leave enough of it to get clarity on the right next steps for their growth. This is critical for a number of reasons. Talking about their issues is helpful and getting clarity is wonderful, but it's not enough. I always get leaders to review out loud the action steps they have chosen to take.

Leaders need to take ownership of their own growth and commit to doing something new about their issue. They must do something they were not doing before. Our role is to come alongside and help them determine what the best next steps would be from their perspective. Then we lovingly hold them accountable for the action steps they choose.

> We never tell leaders what their right next steps should be.

By asking great questions, we help them find the key, simple, doable action steps that will take them forward.

Here are a few questions that help when you are using this final tool in the Mining for Gold process:

- What are a couple of things you could do to move you forward in this issue?
- What do you think would be the most helpful next step here?
- If you could do only one thing this coming week in this area, what would you do?
- Who can you get to help you in this process?

- What other resources would be helpful for you as you move forward?
- How will this action step make a difference for you?
- Who could you call or talk to who would be a great asset to you in this?

It's important not to tell them what they need to do. Help them discover it themselves. As people make their own choices on their next steps, they gain ownership of their own growth and journey. Small steps of obedience lead to a sense of momentum and growth. In time, these leaders will be on their way to a life of thriving.

Deeper-level questions

1. How effective are you in listening deeply to others?
2. What makes a question powerful and transforming?
3. What could you do to cooperate with the Holy Spirit more in developing those around you?
4. Why are practical action steps critical in finding momentum in our development?
5. What could happen if all your leaders were mining for the gold in those around them?

Potential action steps

1. Slow down this week to really listen deeply to the people closest to you.
2. Practise the art of asking great questions. Experiment with different questions.
3. In your conversations, keep the spotlight on the other person and not on yourself. Show interest in that person's life and what God is doing in his or her development.

5. THE WHOLE BODY FULLY ALIVE

Till we all come in the unity of the faith,
and of the knowledge of the Son of God,
unto a perfect man, unto the measure
of the stature of the fulness of Christ

Ephesians 4:13, KJV

Every few minutes he would glance up and scan the horizon, looking for any sign of a spy or band of raiders from the Midianites. When it appeared he was out of sight of his enemies, he would return to his task of threshing out wheat so he and his family could eat. Gideon was nobody's hero. He was just a man doing what he had to do to survive. God saw otherwise.

As he tied up another sack of threshed grain, he looked up and saw a being, appearing more like a heavenly messenger than a man. Gideon felt his heartbeat increase and his fear rise. He likely thought to himself, 'Should I run or defend myself?' For a moment they looked at one another, the angel with a smile and Gideon with an expression of dread. But there was something kind about this visitor.

'The Lord is with you, mighty warrior,' the angel said, with an authority that revealed he was clearly more than a man.

Now Gideon had a smile on his face. 'Yeah, right,' he thought. 'Me, a mighty man of war. That's hilarious.' Gideon knew how timid he was and that he would be Israel's last choice to lead an army.

With all the respect he could muster speaking to this strange, angelic visitor, Gideon pushed back.

'Pardon me, my lord,' Gideon replied, 'but if the LORD is with us, why has all this happened to us? Where are all his wonders that our ancestors told us about when they said, "Did not the LORD bring us up out of Egypt?" But now the LORD has abandoned us and given us into the hand of Midian.'
(Judges 6:13, NIV)

The visitor was not an angel but the Lord God himself. With fire in his eyes and confidence in his words, he said to Gideon, 'Go in the strength you have and save Israel out of Midian's hand. Am I not sending you?' (Judges 6:14, NIV).

'Sending me?' Gideon thought to himself. 'You must have me mixed up with some kind of war hero somewhere. You obviously don't know me and how I'm wired. I am confident I am not your guy.'

Respectfully, for Gideon was always polite and respectful, he again challenged the Lord.

'Pardon me, my lord . . . but how can I save Israel? My clan is the weakest in Manasseh, and I am the least in my family.'

God looked deeply into Gideon's eyes. He waited for a moment so his encouragement to Gideon would hit the mark. This time his words fell more like a prophetic hammer on Gideon's anxious soul.

'I will be with you, and you will strike down all the Midianites, leaving none alive,' God declared.

That is exactly what God did. He walked alongside the timid Gideon, encouraged him and confirmed over and over that he was with him. And, just as God promised, with God beside him, Gideon defeated the Midianites and saved his people from destruction.

I have found that more leaders identify with Gideon than with Moses, David, Esther or Paul. The reason is very simple. We know how anxious and ordinary we feel on most days. We know how timidly and crazily we sometimes act. Sure, we have done some things to help other people, and maybe even gone on a mission trip to serve some needs on far away soil. But honestly, if you asked us to lead in battle and take on an army a hundred times bigger than ours? We would reply, 'Nope, not gonna happen. I'm not your guy or gal.'

It is this dynamic of God using ordinary, anxious and unskilled people to do amazing things that makes Coaching Leadership such an exciting process. God seems to look past the obvious and the qualified to choose the hidden and the unqualified to do his greatest work. He doesn't want to use a few super-gifted and confident people. He wants to use all of us. He wants his whole body to come alive and thrive. He uses ordinary people to do amazing things so the glory goes to him and not to us.

In our churches, businesses and Christian organizations, we can often lose sight of this clear pattern of God: he chooses to use the ordinary and unqualified. We look for the brightest, the most qualified and those with the greatest skills. Like Samuel, we would have chosen Eliab, not David. In many ways we have lost the awe of Christ living in his people. We have forgotten God's pattern to move powerfully through ordinary people. Some of the people we see and work with every day carry treasures inside themselves that would take our breath away. You will have heard the phrase 'Familiarity breeds contempt'. It's true. When we become so familiar with people's patterns and ways, we lose sight of the fact that they carry the greatest treasure of all: 'Christ in [them], the hope of glory' (Colossians 1:27, NIV).

We lose sight of the treasure and the potential God has placed inside ordinary people. We lose our sense of awe in the indwelling Christ in others. It goes deeper too. We sometimes judge the body of Christ as a whole when we see people's immaturity, their apathy and their fears. We are in danger of dismissing Christ's body as hopeless, powerless and un-important, when God sees her as the hope of the world. What a tragedy. The great force in the body of Christ is not us, it is Christ in us!

As we practise Coaching Leadership, we reverse this sad dynamic. We restore the awe and the wonder of this mystery, 'Christ in [people], the hope of glory'. We see the Davids, the Esthers, the Gideons and the Pauls in the everyday Bobs, Marys, Michaels and Johns. We begin to see riches where we couldn't see them before.

Discover the gold in people. Look for it. Hunt for it. Pray God will give you eyes to see it. He loves to answer that prayer. The treasure of Christ in people is stunning. He wants to live powerfully in people in every nation and in every culture on earth. Let's become treasure hunters who can see the gold in his people.

Paul reminds us of Christ's desire to work powerfully through ordinary people:

> Brothers and sisters, think of what you were when you were called. Not many of you were wise by human standards; not many were influential; not many were of noble birth. But God chose the foolish things of the world to shame the wise; God chose the weak things of the world to shame

the strong. God chose the lowly things of this world
and the despised things – and the things that are not –
to nullify the things that are, so that no one may boast
before him.
(1 Corinthians 1:26–29, NIV)

In my tribe of churches, we have a saying we like a lot.
We say that in the kingdom, 'everyone gets to play'. What
we mean is that the work of the kingdom is not for heroes
on the stage but for everyday, ordinary people like us. We
believe that God likes and prefers to use Gideons because his
goal is that people see his power in our weakness. We want
people to learn of his greatness more than the greatness
of man.

My prayer is that we would regain the awe and wonder of
Christ in people. I pray that God would give us eyes to see
deeper, and recognize the potential in the ordinary people
around us as we see them by the power of his Holy Spirit.

The whole body fully alive

And He gave some *as* apostles, and some *as* prophets, and
some *as* evangelists, and some *as* pastors and teachers, for the
equipping of the saints for the work of service, to the building
up of the body of Christ; until we all attain to the unity of the
faith, and of the knowledge of the Son of God, to a mature
man, to the measure of the stature which belongs to the
fullness of Christ. As a result, we are no longer to be children,
tossed here and there by waves and carried about by every
wind of doctrine, by the trickery of men, by craftiness in
deceitful scheming; but speaking the truth in love, we are to
grow up in all *aspects* into Him who is the head, *even* Christ,
from whom the whole body, being fitted and held together by

what every joint supplies, according to the proper working of
each individual part, causes the growth of the body for the
building up of itself in love.
(Ephesians 4:11–16, NASB)

In this powerful scripture, God gives us some key principles
to help us mine for the riches inside the individual members
of Christ's body. Paul tells us that God uses leaders to love,
care for and train the members of his body. Through those
leaders, he shapes ordinary people and organizes them
into an extraordinary community. When those leaders
are freed to do what God created them for, a local body of
people is birthed that paints a living picture of Jesus in that
community.

In Coaching Leadership, we work towards the day when
we all come to the unity of the faith. We labour until *every
member* of Christ's body is *fully alive* with the fullness of
Christ. Paul's instruction to the leadership of the church at
Ephesus is an important description of God's goal for our
Coaching Leadership. As leaders, our role is to develop the
whole body of Christ. God wants every part of Christ's body
to be fully alive and fully functioning. He wants the whole
body to grow up and come into perfect unity so that a fullness
emerges that reflects his fullness.

Coaching Leadership principles do more than mine the
gold in individuals; they work to equip and release whole
communities of people to represent Christ. Imagine each
person in every faith community coming alive and thriving.
Imagine people becoming the treasures God created them to
be, making the contribution God created them to make and
enjoying the love relationship with God and others he created
them to experience. That is corporate thriving. It is a breathtaking possibility.

God wants to show the world the beauty of his mature bride, the body of Christ.

Let's examine some key principles we can glean from Ephesians 4:11–16. These principles will help us as we apply the practice of Coaching Leadership.

- *Every member of the body is important.* God treasures each person and the part he or she plays in building up the body. Every person matters.
- *God uses leaders to build up the body.* Leaders are given for the development of individuals and the whole. These leaders are treasures in themselves. God raises them up to draw out the treasure in others.
- *Every member of the body is called to serve.* Once we learn of the gold we carry, we are to invest it into the work of the kingdom and things that lift up others.
- *God is after maturity in his body.* God has refining processes he uses to purify the gold in us and mature us. He wants a mature body that reflects fully and accurately the greatness of who he is.
- *Maturity in the body leads to greater unity and synergy.* As Christ's nature and character is refined in the individual members of the body, a unified and functioning, complete body emerges. Her beauty increases and God's glory is in full view.
- *A mature body builds itself up.* The gold in every person, when invested in the kingdom, brings a return of growth, more gold and more growth. There is a by-itself dimension to the growth of the body of Christ.
- *A mature body reveals God's fullness.* God's ultimate goal of leadership is to help the body mature so the fullness of Christ is revealed on the earth.

Building a Coaching Leadership culture

One of the questions I get asked most often from leaders and churches is: how do you build a culture of Coaching Leadership in a church or organization? How do you build an empowered culture, where every part does its work and the fullness of Christ comes to life?

The following list includes some of the ways we can cooperate with the process of building a Coaching Leadership culture:

- *Pray.* Ask God to open your eyes so you can see what he sees over your life and the people in your midst. Ask him to restore to you the awe of this reality that Christ lives in us, the hope of glory.
- *Depend on the Holy Spirit.* God is in the people and church-building business. Spiritual gifts require the Spirit to operate. Always remember that Jesus is building his church and he works through the Holy Spirit to do that building. Remember that the Holy Spirit is constantly at work in the lives of people.
- *Be real.* This cannot be faked or manufactured. It is a work of the Spirit of God. True fullness is completely authentic and real. It cannot be a fad or a flavour of the month. It is our lives laid down and surrendered to God daily and receiving all he has planned for us. Allow God to mould and shape you. Be honest about who you are and where you are in your growth process.
- *Be an example.* Empowerment must be modelled. You will reproduce what you are, not what you say. Become empowered yourself. Press into your God-given identity and design. Sow your gifts generously. People see authentic change and real humility when God births it.

Our job is to let God transform us into the image and the instrument he wants to build. Getting coaching is a great step in this process. Model a lifestyle of empowerment and others will follow.

- *Be patient.* This is not a microwave endeavour. Growth and transformation into the image of Christ take time, grace and usually a ton of pressure. We grow slowly through the sanctification process in the hands of the Master Artist. Maturity and unity cannot be rushed. Let God work out his will in his way and in his timing.

- *Mine for gold everywhere and all the time.* Don't settle for running meetings or tracking numbers. See each individual in the body as a gift and a treasure. Get deep into the lives of leaders and individuals. Help them learn to follow and surrender to Christ. The corporate expression of empowerment will come from individuals who are living an empowered life. See beyond people's mistakes and failures. Give them a chance to thrive.

- *Build a culture of grace.* Empowerment comes when the power of Christ flows through every heart. Christ is the essence of grace. His power flows best through weakness, not strength. Allow yourself to be a person in process and give others the freedom to be the same. Grace is God's supernatural power to change everything. Rules don't change people; grace does.

- *Allow all the gifts to play.* Don't empower only the gifts that you enjoy or are most like you. We need a fullness of expression in the body of Christ that allows every type of gift to flourish. We need a sound of fullness that only a full orchestra can bring. Allow the weak and the strong to play. Ask for the Spirit to bring forth his creative power to the music. God is after fullness, not our individual accomplishment.

Deeper-level questions

1. What would it be like to see every member of Christ's body living fully alive?
2. How could you find some Gideons in your local context – men and women who are very human and ordinary, but have a heart for greater things?
3. How much of your time is spent on developing members of the body of Christ?
4. Why is maturity such an important thing for the body of Christ to come into?
5. What impact would a mature body, full of Christ and overflowing, have in your church, business, community or nation?

Potential action steps

1. Pray and ask God for eyes to see any Gideons around you.
2. Take time to study Ephesians 4:11–16 in detail.
3. Ask yourself, 'What would it look like for me to live "fully alive"?'
4. Pray for your family and your church to come alive for God's glory.

6. MULTIPLYING OUR INFLUENCE: INVESTING OUR GOLD WELL

And the things you have heard me say
in the presence of many witnesses entrust
to reliable people who will also be qualified
to teach others.

2 Timothy 2:2, NIV

Think multiplication

The power of the Coaching Leadership process comes alive when we move beyond thinking in terms of our own thriving and choose to help others thrive. We invest ourselves in the gold mining process. I often encourage leaders to think bigger, dream wider and envision larger. God can do much more than we can even think or imagine. He multiplied the loaves and fishes and he can multiply leaders. What could happen if more and more people were set free to flourish?

Something beautiful and powerful takes place when we pray multiplication prayers and pursue multiplication goals. As you come into greater measures of thriving, make a decision to help another person thrive as well. Initiate a few coaching sessions where you can help someone discover their God-given identity and design. As a leader, think every day from a Mining for Gold perspective. Ask God to show you the gold in everyone you meet and for the opportunities to draw out that gold.

Once the leaders you are helping discover the gold they carry, encourage them to invest their gifts in mining for the gold in others. Help them identify simple steps where they can apply Coaching Leadership with someone else. We need to dream big dreams and pursue grand visions, but we also need to break down those visions into manageable next steps we can work on today.

Here are a few thoughts that can lead to multiplying your influence:

- *Invite others to join you.* If you are walking with someone in a study or discipleship process, consider inviting one or two more people to join you. If you are going on a mission trip, pray and invite a key person you sense would greatly benefit from the experience.
- *Invest in multiplication people.* Pray and ask God to identify the key people the Holy Spirit wants you to invest in. Once, Jesus spent all night in prayer and when he came down from the mountain, he chose specific disciples he would pour into and develop.
- *Meet a need as a team.* Look at the needs around your home, church or business and think about who could join you in doing something good and helpful to meet those needs. Do a back-to-school-supplies giveaway. Clean up a dirty park. Tutor some children who need help in school. Ask a neighbour if there's anything you can do to help them.
- *Encourage your leaders to develop other leaders.* Ask all the leaders you are developing to be Mining for Gold in others. Ask them to pass along the blessing by paying it forward in the life of someone else.

- *Listen to people's dreams and desires.* When someone says to you, 'Oh, wow, I've always wanted to do something like that!' – take them up on it. Come alongside them and help them take the first step. Encourage people to do the same with others.

A caution: selfishness with the gifts

There are diversities of gifts, but the same Spirit. There are differences of ministries, but the same Lord. And there are diversities of activities, but it is the same God who works all in all. But the manifestation of the Spirit is given to each one for the profit *of all.*
(1 Corinthians 12:4–7, NKJV)

There is a great danger in this Mining for Gold process. That danger is to consider the riches within God's people as something we can use and manipulate for our own purposes. The members of Christ's body do not belong to us. They belong to God. Their riches are given for the building up of others and the advancement of his kingdom. They are to be invested in God's kingdom enterprise, not ours.

A great wealth of resources will test us. The question God is asking us is this: will we steward the resources and leaders entrusted to us for his kingdom or for ours?

There are two main motives for ministry: agape (selfless love for others) and eros (selfish love that serves our own interests). Both these motives have specific results over time. Selfless, other-centred leadership cares more about the person we are leading than our own welfare. Agape gives us a way of viewing leadership that desires everyone to thrive and prosper. Agape leadership is the way of Jesus and reveals the heart of the Father.

Selfish, eros-motivated leadership is destructive and damaging. Many people have been wounded and crushed by the selfish, fearful leadership actions of those who lead in the church. At times it feels like an epidemic of pain and wreckage.

These are a few examples of selfish leadership:

- *Wanting to look good.* Leaders with this attitude don't care about what's real or true; they only want to appear as if they have their stuff together. Remember Saul in the Old Testament. He begged Samuel to make him look good in front of the people. This is a toxic and dangerous leadership trait.
- *Seeking to always feel good.* This is the source of all sinful indulgence and addiction. Leaders avoid any sense of pain or conflict out of fear of the bad feelings it might bring. Not all of life feels good, but God is always good.
- *Thinking you are always right.* This behaviour is very arrogant and damaging to others. A leader who has a 'be right' disposition sees everyone as below them.
- *Being in control.* Those with a stay-in-control spirit can't stand to see others promoted and blessed. They are constantly working to achieve a certain outcome they have in their minds. Fear and control are the bad roots beneath all these negative leadership traits. We are afraid of things, and then we control to protect ourselves from what we fear. It's a dangerous cycle.
- *Having a hidden agenda.* We hide what we really think and feel about people and situations to help move our agenda forward. We are not truthful and transparent. We are play acting and not entering into real, reciprocal relationships. This trait breaks trust more than any other. We say one thing and do another.

- *Gaining a personal advantage.* We are always climbing, trying to end up ahead of or above others. We are not afraid to step on someone along the road to our goals. We are not for the good of others; we are trying to see how things can be good for us. This is a tremendously selfish leadership trait.
- *Choosing to remain undisturbed.* This is when leaders avoid changing at any cost. Their walls of self-protection are so thick they can't conceive of changing their ways, much less repenting for their sin. This trait is subtle and harder to pin down. But it is destructive and keeps us in an immature leadership flow.[1]

Invest your talents

Coaching Leadership is focused on the well-being of others. Coaching leaders pour out the talents and treasures they have for the good of others. They don't fear being generous with their time and talents. They invest their best and take risks to help others. It is a mindset and a lifestyle of love.

> And he who had received the five talents came forward, bringing five talents more, saying, 'Master, you delivered to me five talents; here, I have made five talents more.' His master said to him, 'Well done, good and faithful servant. You have been faithful over a little; I will set you over much. Enter into the joy of your master.'
> (Matthew 25:20–21, ESV)

God placed his treasure inside you for a purpose: so that you could invest it in his kingdom. Our gifts, our love, our efforts

---

1 Bob Mumford, *Agape Road: Journey to Intimacy with the Father* (Destiny Image Publishers, 2006), pp. 104–105.

must be invested in the good of others. In the parable above, Jesus tells us where we should invest our most valuable resources: in his kingdom.

> Coaching Leadership is about helping people make the contribution God created them to make.

The gold and gifts inside people were given for the good of all. We don't own our lives or our gifts. All we have, we have received. Our role is to be faithful stewards over all God has entrusted to us.

As leaders learn how to sow and reap, they enter into the powerful dynamic of this parable. God wants to entrust more to us, but he wisely doesn't do so until he is sure we are mature enough to handle it all. That is the power of this parable. Our gold is a resource God wants to invest somewhere. Take the time to pray and seek him to learn where he wants to invest the treasures inside you.

Deeper-level questions

1. How would a multiplication mindset change the way you practise leadership?
2. What would it look like for you to invest your time and talents into the critical task of developing thriving, godly leaders?
3. How does selfishness keep you from developing the leaders around you?
4. What areas of your time and leadership need to change so you can invest more in developing leaders?
5. Why is developing coaching leaders a multiplication type of activity?

Potential action steps

1. Look around you. Identify the leaders who have the capacity to raise up other leaders.
2. Stop and think about whether you are operating from an addition or a multiplication mindset.
3. Choose someone in whom you see leadership potential and invite them to walk more closely with you as you lead.

Part 2

GOD'S REFINING PROCESS: SIX PRINCIPLES THAT LEAD TO THRIVING

7. THE HOLY SPIRIT DOES THE WORK OF REFINING

The righteous shall flourish like a palm tree,
He shall grow like a cedar in Lebanon.
Those who are planted in the house of the LORD
Shall flourish in the courts of our God.
They shall still bear fruit in old age;
They shall be fresh and flourishing,
To declare that the LORD is upright;
He is my rock, and *there is* no unrighteousness
in Him.

Psalm 92:12–15, NKJV

Refined to thrive

God's ultimate goal in the refining process is to bring forth thriving, godly leaders for his kingdom purposes. His refining leads to our thriving. In God, refining is never random. He has a specific purpose for every leader's life and he knows how to bring each one into it. He wants to reveal Jesus through us. God sees the gold in us, draws out that gold and then refines it so we bear fruit. Although God's refining processes are not always gentle or painless, we rest in the knowledge that his heart and motives are always good towards us. God's refining is not punishment. It is rooted in love.

What does a thriving leader look like?

The scripture from Psalm 92 gives us some clues as to what it means to thrive from God's perspective. God refines us so that we may enjoy his life, flourish and bear fruit. As coaching leaders, there are several important lessons for us to glean from these verses. We see five things that are happening in the life of a thriving leader:

1. *They flourish.* To flourish means to grow or develop in a healthy, vigorous way. Thriving leaders are always growing. As loved sons and daughters they are full of life and overflowing.
2. *They are planted.* Thriving leaders do not drift through life searching for a home. They put down roots and build deep and lasting relationships. They give and receive love in community.
3. *They do God's work.* They flourish in his courts. They do his kingdom work. They commit themselves to seeking his kingdom and his righteousness first.
4. *They bear fruit throughout their lives.* Their fruit begins when they first come to faith in Christ, and it matures and multiplies throughout their lifetime. They bear fruit into old age.
5. *They are continually renewed.* Their leaves are green and full. They encounter God constantly, bringing freshness and renewal through every season of their life.

Mining for Gold is about multiplying thriving, godly leaders in every place. Just as natural mining is challenging and takes specific technical skills, so too does Coaching Leadership. There is gold in the people all around us. We must have eyes to see it, and learn to draw it out. Let's remember our acrostic, GOLD, which is the core of Coaching Leadership:

- *Gold is everywhere.* Godly, thriving leaders are scarce, but the raw matcrial for developing those leaders is everywhere.
- *Open your eyes to see it.* To identify the true potential God has placed in leaders, we need to see them through the eyes of the Spirit.
- *Learn the skills to draw it out.* We must put in the hard work to learn Coaching Leadership and increase our competency in developing leaders.
- *Develop others continuously.* One of our greatest contributions as leaders is to leave a legacy of godly, thriving leaders.

In this second section of *Mining for Gold*, we will look at six principles that help leaders thrive. As Coaching Leaders, we must study and understand these principles to thrive personally. Then we must turn our attention to others to help them thrive. The six principles are at the core of God's refining process. To cooperate with God's refining, we need to grasp these principles and begin to apply them in our Coaching Leadership.

The six principles of thriving

1. *The Holy Spirit does the work of refining.* He brings forth the gold. He helps people thrive. The Spirit does the heavy lifting. We simply learn to cooperate with him.
2. *Our true identity is the foundation of thriving.* Truth sets us free. We learn the truth about who God is and who we are in his Word. When we know God in truth, we begin to understand the truth about ourselves. He is our perfect, loving Father. We are his beloved sons and daughters. God created us with a purpose. To know Jesus deeply is eternal life. It is the essence of thriving.

3. *We thrive when we cooperate with our God-given design.*
   Our design gives us clues as to the purpose God created
   us for. A divine wind and momentum come when we
   cooperate with how we are designed. When we live
   from our design, we encounter a river of thriving,
   a supernatural flow. Life and ministry become more
   like sailing and less like rowing.

4. *Each of us has a sweet spot: the place we most naturally
   bear fruit.* The sweet spot is the key that opens the
   door to thriving. It is our natural place of fruit-bearing.
   When we bear much fruit, God gets much glory
   (John 15:8). Our ministry flows naturally from our
   sweet spot.

5. *The cross: God's great refining tool.* The cross is critical
   to thriving because, in the kingdom, death leads to
   life. We must pay attention to our struggles and
   pain. God uses suffering and difficulty to conform
   us to Christ's image. We must listen to where God
   is calling us to die so that we may live. Death and
   resurrection are at the heart of God's refining and
   how we are transformed and renewed throughout
   our lives.

6. *All true thriving is relational.* To love God and others
   is God's great desire for all of us. We are to become
   great at receiving and giving love to others.
   Relationships are at the core of our life in Christ.

There is tremendous depth and breadth in all six of these
principles. We can't dive into the heart of them all in one
book. Take time to pray, ponder and pursue them in all their
fullness. Remember, the six principles are about helping
leaders thrive. Coaching Leadership is built on the foundation
of these six principles.

Thriving principle #1: the Holy Spirit does the work of refining

The work of developing leaders is ultimately God's job, not ours. As coaching leaders, we are God's assistants as he does this critical work. Scores of leadership development books and resources emphasize the things we need to do to train and equip leaders. Methods and training programmes are important, but God himself is the ultimate leader developer. He does the heavy lifting. He does the moulding and shaping, not us.

In Coaching Leadership, we celebrate that God is in charge of developing leaders. It takes the pressure off us. We don't produce growth. God does. Our role as coaching leaders is to come alongside leaders, as Barnabas did with Paul, and help them cooperate with what the Holy Spirit is doing in their lives. We help them discern where the Father is working so they can join him.

The Holy Spirit has his own school of leadership. It is a living and dynamic school that happens in real life, with real people, in real time. God uses formal leadership training programmes. He uses classes, podcasts, sermons and schools, but these resources are not the ultimate developer of leaders: the Holy Spirit is. He uses the classes, teachings, sermons, mentors and materials, along with real-life experiences, to shape and mould a thriving leader. God's Spirit works every minute of every day and through every season of our lives to bring us into thriving. He mines the gold in us and then takes personal responsibility to refine that gold.

Peter: a leader refined by the Holy Spirit

In the Gospels and the book of Acts, we find one of the fullest pictures of refining in the life of Peter. As Jesus calls Peter and begins to develop him, we see a leader transformed from an impulsive, rough fisherman into a mighty preacher of truth. God changed him from a frightened disciple who denied Jesus three times and re-formed him into a bold witness who spoke and lived fearlessly. How did all this happen? God himself, through the work of the Holy Spirit, mined and refined Peter's life so that he was brought forth as gold.

In Jesus' masterful hands, Peter came into the fullness of who he was created to be so that he could walk into the fullness of what he was created to do. Through God's refining process, God separates the gold from the ore in every leader's life. This is what he does best: he redeems and restores men and women so they bring forth the gold of Christ's nature. In God's hands, we bear the fruit we were designed to bear.

From the first day Jesus met Peter, he could see the nuggets of gold in Peter's life. Beginning with his encounter at Peter's boat on the shores of the Sea of Galilee, Jesus knew the purpose and plan for Peter's life. He saw the gold in Peter and knew he needed to draw it out.

Here are some of the indicators that told Jesus there was gold waiting to be discovered in Peter:

- *His obedience.* Jesus saw Peter's willingness to leave his occupation of fishing to follow him completely. Peter would learn to become a fisher of men.
- *His declaration.* Peter declared with simple faith that Jesus was the Christ, the Messiah, the Son of the living God.
- *His speech.* Peter frequently served in the role of spokesman for the disciples in their interaction with Jesus.
- *His zeal.* Peter's burning passion was to see God's kingdom come and his will done.

- *His relationships.* Peter was in a deep trust relationship with Jesus so that he was included in Jesus' inner circle along with James and John.
- *His influence.* Leadership is influence and Peter had an impact upon the other disciples and their decisions.
- *His faith.* Peter was the only one to walk on water when the rest of the disciples trembled in the boat with fear.

These were the nuggets of gold that Jesus saw in his fiery disciple. Yet there were also clear signs of weakness and dross, fleshly behaviours that were a part of Peter's complex inner world. This is the reality of our refining process. We have inside us both the gold of God's nature and the dross of our earthly nature.

Look at a few aspects of Peter's fleshly nature:

- *His impulsiveness.* His passion would sometimes rule him. Cutting off the ear of the high priest's servant is a good example.
- *His overconfidence.* Peter resists Jesus. Right after his great declaration of Jesus' divinity, Peter says that Jesus should never be put to death as an atoning sacrifice.
- *His weakness.* He falls asleep with the other disciples in the Garden of Gethsemane right before Jesus is betrayed.
- *His fear.* He infamously denies that he even knows the Saviour. This was Peter's greatest personal failure.
- *His pride.* He argues with the other disciples about who would be the greatest in the kingdom of God. As with many dynamic leaders, Peter struggled with selfish ambition.

God knows we have both gold and dross within us. He knew that Pentecost was coming for Peter and he needed to prepare him for it. God sees our future and is working to bring us towards it so we can fulfil our assignments and finish our race. He uses a refining process to separate the flesh from the spirit in each of us. As it was for Peter, that process can be painful, long and heated, but the results are beautiful, like seeing Peter preaching powerfully on the day of Pentecost. God does his leader development work masterfully.

Give the leader development process back to the Holy Spirit

Coaching Leadership works as we come in humility and submit ourselves to the leadership of the Holy Spirit. The Holy Spirit sees the gold and the dross in each of us. With skill and compassion, he does the work of teaching, training, convicting and restoring us as we journey towards thriving and maturity. His great desire is to reveal Jesus through our lives. Our role is to partner with the Holy Spirit as he does his work of refining. It's up to us to help leaders discern where God is working in their lives, what he might be doing and to help them cooperate with him.

This list looks at seven things the Holy Spirit does in the leadership development process:

1. *He teaches us and guides us.* He is the Spirit of truth. He teaches us truth from the Word and from our experiences. He also teaches us through mentors and other leaders in our lives. The Spirit knows exactly what is needed in each leader to help him or her mature and bear fruit.

    However, when He, the Spirit of truth, has come, He will guide you into all truth; for He will not speak on

His own *authority*, but whatever He hears He will speak;
and He will tell you things to come.
(John 16:13, NKJV)

2. *He comforts us.* Life can be hard, and refining can get
   very uncomfortable. When the heat gets too hot, the
   Spirit comforts us with tender compassion. Jesus called
   him the Comforter. When our refining process is at its
   most painful, the Holy Spirit draws nearest to help us
   move through the pain into thriving.

   But when the Comforter comes, whom I shall send to you
   from the Father, the Spirit of truth who proceeds from the
   Father, He will testify of Me.
   (John 15:26, NKJV)

3. *He empowers us.* The Holy Spirit gives us the strength,
   grace and power to live out the divine call on our lives.
   He fills us with the life of Jesus so that we are bold and
   do things we could never do on our own.

   But you will receive power when the Holy Spirit has
   come upon you, and you will be my witnesses in
   Jerusalem and in all Judea and Samaria, and to the end
   of the earth.
   (Acts 1:8, ESV)

4. *He glorifies Jesus.* The Spirit continually points us
   to Jesus, who is at work in us. Jesus was the one who
   refined Peter, and he is refining us. The Spirit reveals
   to us where Jesus is working. He shows us the
   magnificence and sufficiency of Christ in everything
   and in every circumstance.

He will glorify Me, for He will take of what is Mine and
declare *it* to you.
(John 16:14, NKJV)

5. *He convicts us.* He reveals to us our sin, so we can repent.
The Holy Spirit brings conviction and shows us what is
gold and what is dross. He shows us what is flesh and
what is Spirit in us.

Nevertheless I tell you the truth. It is to your advantage
that I go away; for if I do not go away, the Helper will
not come to you; but if I depart, I will send Him to you.
And when He has come, He will convict the world of sin,
and of righteousness, and of judgment.
(John 16:7–8, NKJV)

6. *He gives us life.* The Spirit gives life. He restores us when
we are empty and spent. When we experience the cross
and come through, he pours out resurrection life. He
renews us throughout our lifetime and keeps our leaves
fresh and green.

But if the Spirit of Him who raised Jesus from the dead
dwells in you, He who raised Christ from the dead will
also give life to your mortal bodies through His Spirit
who dwells in you.
(Romans 8:11, NKJV)

7. *He brings us back to our Father.* The foundation of thriving
is our love relationship with our Father God. Wherever
we are separated or wounded in our relationship with
God as our Father, the Holy Spirit will work to restore
that relationship with him. He is the Spirit of adoption

who helps us come as beloved sons and daughters to Abba, which means 'Daddy' in Aramaic. We are heirs with Christ, his brothers and sisters, in God's family. The Spirit awakens our spirit to the truth that we are God's treasured children.

> For as many as are led by the Spirit of God, these are sons of God. For you did not receive the spirit of bondage again to fear, but you received the Spirit of adoption by whom we cry out, 'Abba, Father.' The Spirit Himself bears witness with our spirit that we are children of God, and if children, then heirs – heirs of God and joint heirs with Christ.
> (Romans 8:14–17, NKJV)

All these works of the Holy Spirit are critical in the refining process. Refining is about conforming us to the image of Christ, and the Spirit takes the lead role in this important process. God's goal for our lives is to conform us to the image of his Son. He wants us to become like Jesus; to reflect nothing less than pure Jesus. As gold goes through an intense and super-heated process to become pure, so it is with us. Disappointment, failure, betrayal, delay and dashed dreams are all part of the refining process. The Holy Spirit is with us in every one of those critical times. At times we don't feel as if we'll make it. The heat is too hot. Our inner world seems to be coming apart. All of that is in God's hands, a part of his refining process. The gold of Christ's image in us must be separated from the dross of our flesh. A life of ease and comfort doesn't conform us to the nature of Christ. The heat of difficulty and pain does, and the Holy Spirit is present through it all.

When gold has been fully purified, it carries the highest value it will ever possess. It's the same with us. As the character of Christ is revealed in us in purity, we bear much fruit, and God gets glory. That is the true nature of flourishing.

Sailing vs rowing

Flourishing is not a work of man or of the flesh. It is a work of the Spirit. Many times in life and leadership, we feel as if we are in a rowing boat, pulling ourselves across life's ocean to some distant future. Waves and wind beat against us and we feel exhausted. Our hands are hurting with blisters and we are not sure we can make it any further. There is a better way. Rowing represents leading out of self-effort. God wants to send the wind of his Spirit to help us get to where we are going.

In Psalm 92 we see a leader filled with God's life. The Divine Wind is filling, moulding and flowing through him. If you invite the Holy Spirit in prayer and constant dependence, he will do amazing things in your leadership development. I have seen the Holy Spirit work powerfully in countless Coaching Leadership sessions. As we seek his wisdom and guidance in a leader's life, again and again he shows us what the Father is doing and how the leader can join him. He highlights the important things God is doing so the leader has clarity and knows what to do next.

To live a Coaching Leadership lifestyle, we must walk in constant dependence on, and moment-by-moment obedience to, the Holy Spirit. Mining for Gold works through intimate cooperation with the Holy Spirit. We must give the leadership development process back to the only one capable of getting the job done: the Spirit of God.

What is the power source of your life and leadership development efforts? Have you learned to let the Spirit work on your behalf? Are you trusting him to do the work, or are you trying to develop leaders in your own strength? Are you trusting in the latest fad or technique to develop leaders? There is a better way. Walk side by side with leaders, trust in the Holy Spirit and help them take the next steps in their journey of faithful obedience.

Jesus told his disciples before he returned to the Father to wait for the 'Promise of the Father', the Spirit, to come and help them. He knew they had a monumental task in front of them, so he gave them a gift powerful enough to help them accomplish it: a mighty infilling of the Person of the Holy Spirit. God's Spirit became the source and the agency that would propel the mission of the kingdom forward and accomplish all the amazing works that God planned to do through the apostles. Their job was to wait and surrender to the Spirit.

God is offering us that same power today. He loves to give us his power in place of our weakness. He loves pouring out his strength through weak people so that he gets the glory.

Sailing is a more biblical picture for our life with God. In sailing, there is an outside force, the wind of God's Spirit, helping us do things we could never do on our own. The Spirit does the work. He can move a mighty ship through the water with ease and beauty, but that ship must cooperate with the Wind. He is able to accomplish things that are impossible for us to do in our own effort.

Your role is to orientate your life and leadership to where you see the wind of the Spirit blowing. Your task is to discern where God is leading you and let his Spirit work powerfully to get you there. His Spirit knows the destination and the path, and has the power to propel you all the way.

Quit trying to do everything yourself. Press into the Person of the Holy Spirit. Lay down any fear, striving and control you have, and let the river of his life flow to you and through you. The life of the Spirit is a life of growth, peace, unceasing joy and adventure: 'For the kingdom of God is not a matter of eating and drinking but of righteousness and peace and joy in the Holy Spirit' (Romans 14:17, ESV).

Developing leaders is not all up to you. God wants to do his amazing work of Mining for Gold with you and through you. Let the Spirit of God bring about the will of God and the fruit of God in your leadership. Orientate your sails to where you discern God is working in a leader's life and enjoy the ride. It's a fun and exciting adventure to cooperate with God as he shapes a leader for his kingdom.

Deeper-level questions

1. What would flourishing look like for you personally?
2. How would you describe your relationship with the Holy Spirit?
3. What aspects of the Holy Spirit's work can help you the most as you develop leaders?
4. Does your life and ministry feel more like sailing or rowing?
5. How could cooperating more closely with the Holy Spirit change the impact of your life and leadership?

Potential action steps

1. Honestly assess whether you are flourishing or just surviving.
2. Study the Person and work of the Holy Spirit. Invite him to teach you who you are and what God has called you to do.
3. Pray before all your Coaching Leadership discussions with leaders so that you are always dialled into the heartbeat of the Spirit for others.

8. OUR TRUE IDENTITY IS THE FOUNDATION OF THRIVING

> For all who are led by the Spirit of God are sons of
> God. For you did not receive the spirit of slavery to
> fall back into fear, but you have received the Spirit of
> adoption as sons, by whom we cry, 'Abba! Father!'

> Romans 8:14–15, ESV

Thriving sons and daughters

One of our major roles in Coaching Leadership is helping leaders find their true identity as sons and daughters of God. Identity is the foundation of thriving. Our identity in Christ is a solid and enduring core inside us. Our identity is the secure place within us from which we deal with life and our relationships. When our identity in the Father is secure, we feel at home and at rest wherever we are. When our identity in Christ is weak or broken, we sense we're adrift and uncentred. Without a secure identity, life feels out of sync and scattered. When we are secure in our identity, we have a growing sense of authority because we know who we are and *whose* we are. When our identity is secure, we can say with Paul: 'nevertheless I am not ashamed, for I know whom I have believed and am persuaded that He is able to keep what I have committed to Him until that Day' (2 Timothy 1:12, NKJV).

Like Paul, we can have confidence in who God is and who
we are. When we are secure as sons and daughters, we better
steward our Father's resources and blessings. Identity is at the
core of who we are and at the core of thriving. Let's learn
how it works.

In the beginning God made man in his image.

> [27]So God created man in His own image;
> in the image of God He created him;
> male and female He created them.
> [28]Then God blessed them, and God said to them, 'Be fruitful
> and multiply; fill the earth and subdue it; have dominion over
> the fish of the sea, over the birds of the air, and over every
> living thing that moves on the earth.'
> (Genesis 1:27–28, NKJV)

Three key components of our identity are revealed in these
verses.

1. *We are created in God's image (verse 27).* We reflect him
   and who he is. We are made with intentional design
   to reflect our Creator God.
2. *We are created to thrive (verse 28).* God wants us to be
   fruitful and multiply. His great desire for each of us
   is to come alive and live fruitfully. This is a critical truth.
   Thriving is not just for some people; it is for every
   person created in his image.
3. *We are created with a purpose (verse 28).* Our purpose
   is to multiply and fill the earth with God's life and
   goodness. We are born to reveal him on the earth. We
   carry his image, we reflect him and we are his treasured
   possession. As we live in dynamic, loving relationship
   with God, the world will come to know him.

Our identity in Christ gives us the confidence and freedom to discover what God has created us to do. To thrive, we must begin with who we are, then move towards what we are to do. Being always precedes doing. The discovery of our identity is the key that unlocks the door to our future.

Let's examine how identity shapes and forms how we view God, ourselves and our place in this world.

Knowing God

When we first receive the indwelling life of Christ, a dramatic transformation takes place. We become brand new sons and daughters of the King of all creation. We become carriers, hosts of the living presence of Christ, earthen vessels carrying immense treasure. That is our true identity. We are not accidents, mistakes or hopeless failures. In time, as we mature into thriving sons and daughters, others see God and his nature coming through us.

For many years I served God with all my strength, but had no clarity around my identity. I lacked a solid internal picture of God's goodness and love for me. Not knowing God's true nature left me insecure and striving. I was continually stressed about many things. I worried about my relationships, my future, my past and what to do with my life. I was always unsure of which path I should take.

Without a clear identity, I lived from one task to the next, struggling to make sense of everything. Anxiety and stress were constant burdens. My relationships were strained because I didn't know how to receive love from God or share his love with others. I didn't know I was loved, so I could not love others well. Life didn't make much sense. Although I had given my life to Christ, I still lacked a deep heart connection with Christ himself. Thriving was an elusive mystery to me.

I had not learned how to draw from the immense goodness of God. I had not learned to relate to God as a loved son.

> Knowing God is the foundation of knowing ourselves.

God's nature and his goodness reveal so many things about who we are and how the world works. Our first step in thriving is to know God in all his beauty and fullness. Jesus said, 'Now this is eternal life: that they know you, the only true God, and Jesus Christ, whom you have sent' (John 17:3, NIV).

Jesus told us that life at its core is knowing God.

One of the key ways we come to know God is through the Scriptures. The Word of God reveals the nature of God to us. In the Word, we discover he is gracious and compassionate, slow to anger and abounding in love. We learn of his steadfast love for us and his faithfulness to all mankind.

Our relationship with God must move beyond information *about* God to an intimate walk *with* God. We need to know him deeply, from the heart. Our role is to ask, seek and knock on every door to find out more about him. At our core, we need to know the true nature, character and goodness of God. Dive into the depths of God's love and power. Study the Scriptures and all the wonderful books on God's greatness. Listen to teaching on his incredible faithfulness. Knowing God helps you discover who you are.

Spend some time in focused prayer asking the Father to reveal himself to you in intimate reality. Read his Word and listen for his voice. Wait for fresh revelation about his heart for you. He desires to reveal himself to you in all his fullness. As you begin to know God at deeper and deeper levels, you will be transformed.

Knowing God more deeply is a glorious unfolding. Knowing his strength gives you strength. Discovering his compassion fills you with compassion. Learning his wisdom fills you with wisdom. Understanding his authority increases your authority. To truly thrive, you must enter a lifetime of discovering more and more about the amazing God we love and serve. It is a rewarding search that never ends.

Our faithful, loving Father

What makes our identity in Christ so secure is that it never changes. God is always the same in every season. He is always a loving Father and we are always his loved sons and daughters. Regardless of what you are experiencing or feeling, God is always loving, always kind, always generous. He is your perfect Father who loves you with an eternal, perfect love.

God's love is not fickle. He doesn't change his perspective on us depending on the things we do. He loves us completely on our worst day as much as he does on our best day. He constantly looks for ways to be good to us and help us. His love is fixed. It doesn't change with the seasons or with our behaviour. That truth settles our hearts. That truth blows me away.

Knowing that God loves me so completely shapes the way I see myself.

> And we have known and believed the love that God has for us. God is love, and he who abides in love abides in God, and God in him.
> (1 John 4:16, NKJV)

God is love. He is not just loving; he is love itself. It is not enough to know intellectually that God loves you. You must believe he loves you unconditionally and completely. His love is the bedrock truth upon which we build lives of meaning and purpose. The Greek word for God's love in the Bible is *agape*. Agape was a new word at the time the New Testament was written. It describes a love that is so wonderful it could not have come from this world. Agape comes only from God himself, because he is agape.

It sometimes helps to have a visual picture to understand the love of God.

Agape
Eternal, unbroken,
sacrificial love

Eros
Self-serving love

Figure 1: God's love vs human love

God's love can be depicted like the image in Figure 1: a straight arrow. He loves us without condition; without a hook in it. God loves us, wanting and needing nothing in return. Love flows from him to us like the flow of a river.

Our human love, on the other hand, looks like the hooked arrow in Figure 1. It is often self-seeking and self-referential. We love people but with conditions. We love, wanting something in return.

I like these two arrows because they make clear the two ways we can love others and lead people. We can lead with God's unfailing, unconditional love, or we can lead with a selfish, conditional love, trying to get what we want from people and situations.

Agape can be defined as eternal, unbroken, sacrificial benevolence. God has always loved and will always love you. His love flows continuously from his incredible heart. He is ready to lavish his love on you right now. He loves you when you are good and when you are bad. He loves you when you succeed and when you fail miserably. In his love, he is always working things for your good, even the painful things. In his love, he has good plans for you that he wants to bring you into.

Agape is pure goodness that flows eternally from the Trinity to people. It originates in God and flows from him to us. We cannot create it or work it up. We cannot earn it. It is his eternal, magnificent gift to us, his sons and daughters. Nothing can separate us from this unfailing love. Agape can only be received from God and given away.

God's love is like an unfailing waterfall of pure goodness, flowing from his heart and pouring over our lives every minute of every day. And his love never stops flowing to us. I like to imagine myself standing with my arms outstretched underneath a rushing waterfall of his unfailing love. I can picture myself drinking in the fullness of that love – his love healing, changing and transforming me.

Right now, you can place yourself by faith underneath the flow of that waterfall of benevolent goodness. By faith, you can trust that God loves you with an unfailing love. By faith you can receive a fresh infilling of the love of God. There is no limit to the supply of God's love for you. You could fill a million swimming pools full of God's love and it would be like taking a teaspoon of water from the ocean. You receive God's love by believing in it by faith.

Our hearts need continuous fresh revelation about how much we are loved. Our identity forms, grows and expands as we mature in our understanding of the love God has for us. The power of his love can change the way we think, the choices we make and the way we relate to others.

Love changes *us*.

In 1 Corinthians 13:4–8, God's love is described in this way:

Love is patient, love is kind. It does not envy, it does not boast, it is not proud. It does not dishonour others, it is not self-seeking, it is not easily angered, it keeps no record of wrongs. Love does not delight in evil but rejoices with the truth. It always protects, always trusts, always hopes, always perseveres. Love never fails.

(NIV)

Paul's beautiful description of love is a poetic masterpiece. It captures the selfless beauty of the love of God.

This is the face of agape. Reading this passage, we can see what love looks like and how it acts. These attributes of agape are the essence of our Father's heart towards us. Such truths nourish our hearts and help them come alive and begin to thrive. Like the nutrients that a tree draws from rich soil, agape brings fresh nutrients of truth and grace to the heart that receives it by faith.

Agape is not temporal or trendy. God's love has always been from the beginning and it will endure eternally. He is love itself and he is the same yesterday, today and for ever. We need God's unfailing love like we need oxygen. Paul prayed in Ephesians 3:16–19:

that out of his glorious riches he may strengthen you with power through his Spirit in your inner being, so that Christ may dwell in your hearts through faith. And I pray that you, being rooted and established in love, may have power, together with all the Lord's holy people, to grasp how wide and long and high and deep is the love of Christ, and to know this love that surpasses knowledge – that you may be filled to the measure of all the fullness of God.

(NIV)

That is a description of thriving. A leader rooted and grounded in love is positioned like a healthy tree to thrive and bear much fruit. Leaders need to grow and understand the depths of God's love as revelation, not just information. If we spent our whole lives studying agape and earned five PhDs in love, we would still be in kindergarten in our understanding of it. We need daily fresh revelations of his love to come into the fullness of what he has for us.

Knowing God as the perfect loving Father is the doorway to thriving. If we don't see him correctly, our hearts will forever struggle with lies that tell us we are less than, and undeserving of, his love. When we see him as he is, we will see ourselves as we truly are: beloved sons and daughters.

Hindrances to our true identity

When our identity is rooted in something other than God's unfailing love, we struggle to find the rest that leads to thriving. We live more as orphans than sons and daughters.

Here are some false things we can be rooted in that keep us from thriving:

- *Performance.* We can stress and strive to do something important so we will feel worthy of love.
- *Self-righteousness.* Like the Pharisees Jesus dealt with, we can become full of our own sense of 'rightness' and self-importance. Instead of living from a tender, grateful heart, we become arrogant and condescending.
- *Pleasure.* Whether it's drugs, alcohol, pornography or entertainment, we become handcuffed to our idols of feeling good. Our greatest motive becomes avoiding pain or covering it up with anything that helps us feel better.
- *Shame.* Knowing the bad things we have done, we can live under a heavy weight of shame and oppression.

We don't just feel bad, we believe that we are bad.
Not understanding the gospel of grace, we can be
completely cut off from the sin-freeing power of the
grace of God. Carrying shame and guilt is like carrying
a backpack full of smelly bricks. It stinks and it's
extremely heavy. The weight keeps us from running
freely towards a life of thriving.

- *Fear.* Because we've experienced pain and loss, fear can
  take root in our soul. We become afraid of what we
  might do wrong or what others may do to us. Fear can
  feel like a constant draining tension, or a debilitating
  tidal wave. We can be overcome by panic and a constant
  dread of the future. When we live in fear, we are in
  chains, unable to run free.

- *Control.* Fear ultimately leads to control. We feel that
  if we can get every detail of our lives to work out just
  right, everything will fall into place. We control by
  withdrawing from others to protect ourselves. We
  can never relax because there are so many factors to
  consider and so many details to fix. Control gives us
  an illusion of thriving. The truth is that we are not in
  control; we have never been in control. God is in control
  and wants to be the Director and the loving Leader of
  every detail of our lives.

- *A victim mindset.* We can feel that we are always
  powerless, adrift on the sea of others' choices and
  decisions. This is a terrible identity killer, because
  we give up our God-given power to make decisions
  and make changes for the future.

- *Ruled by flesh and sin.* We can be bound to addictions,
  pleasures and our own will. We are living as orphans
  and eating the scraps of life instead of God's rich
  bounty.

Jesus came to set us free from all these false sources of identity. When he shows us our true identity as loved sons and daughters, our hearts begin to relax. When he frees us from fear, we begin to let our roots grow down into the Father's love. Thriving only manifests from a deep sense of rest. Truth about God's love sets us free to rest.

These false sources come from an orphan mentality. I lived with an orphan mentality for decades. It is an empty cup. When we live with an orphan mentality, we struggle to come into the rest and security our hearts need. Our inner world speaks to us with thoughts like this:

- I'm on my own. No-one is there for me.
- It's all up to me. I have to take care of everything myself.
- I can't trust others.
- I'm guilty and judged because I am so sinful.
- I have nothing and I always live in lack.
- I don't know the way forward.
- No-one is there to help me and guide me in my journey.
- I can't seem to discover the life of abundance.
- I live stressed, anxious and unsatisfied because I have to control everything.
- Deep inside, I'm terribly afraid of failure, rejection and being alone.

Loved sons and daughters think differently. They know the foundation of their Father's faithful care. Fear has been driven out by love. In faith, they lie back and relax, letting God's goodness and blessing flow to them. They don't have to find blessings; blessings are continuously finding them. They grow in grace and love, and enjoy the rest that God provides.

Sons and daughters have these thoughts:

- God likes me, accepts me, cares about me and wants to be good to me.
- God is watching over me so I am not alone in this world.
- I can relax.
- I am safe, protected and secure in my place as his child.
- God will make a way for me. I don't have to make everything happen.
- The pressure is off. It's all up to God, not me.
- I'm forgiven, free, accepted and righteous in God's sight.
- I can come freely at any time into his presence to get the wisdom, guidance and help that I need.
- I have an abundance. My Father owns it all. I don't have to be jealous of others' blessings or successes. My Dad has more than enough for whatever I need.
- I don't have to fear tomorrow. My future is secure.
- I can rest, enjoy life and live in peace.
- I can face my broken places, get help and find healing.

We can rest when we learn our true identity because we no longer live from self-effort. We have a continuous source of strength and peace. Rest becomes a normal part of our life. We are restful and peaceful regardless of the outward circumstances we are facing. We rest and draw strength from God every day and at any time.

Our focus becomes less and less on self and what we need. We begin to notice and care about the needs of others. We can start pouring love into those around us out of the overflow of love we are experiencing. The common characteristic of leaders who know their true identity is selflessness. They start to live like Jesus, pouring their hearts and gifts into blessing others. Loving well is the opposite of selfish striving. Love leads us to give our lives away in blessing others.

Believing the truth which sets us free

The chains that bind us to a false identity are the lies we believe. We have grown up in a world flooded with sin, hardship and pain. Hard things come into all our lives. The devil, just as he did in the garden with our ancestors, Adam and Eve, lies to us. He takes our painful experiences and plants lies into the soil of our hearts and minds.

These lies are like poison to our soul. They make us sick. They begin to build in us a false identity. We start to believe things like this:

- I'll never amount to anything.
- No-one will ever be there for me.
- People like me never get a break.
- I don't have what it takes to succeed.
- I am always on my own when I have to work things out.
- I'm too broken to be loved.

When we believe lies, they become chains that bind us. We find ourselves in a prison of our own false beliefs. Jesus said, 'Then you will know the truth, and the truth will set you free' (John 8:32, NIV). We need truth like we need oxygen.

To break the power of lies, we need to be relentless with our passion for truth. We cannot thrive if we are not free, and we cannot be free unless we are walking in truth.

So how do we escape lies and live in the freedom of truth?

We allow God to have access to our inner world. The key to truth is humility. Humility opens the door to truth. When we stay stuck in our pride or self-righteousness, we stay bound. If you come to God in humility, he will reveal his truth to you to set you free. His truth will come and destroy the web of lies you have believed.

Humility leads to repentance. When we repent, we turn from our false way of thinking and embrace the reality of what God says is true. Truth is not information. Truth is a person. Truth is the wisdom of God found in the Person of Jesus Christ.

Allowing Christ access to my thinking, my emotions, my relationships and my calendar opens the door for his transforming power to work in me. Christ lives to bring us into the fullness of our relationship with the Father. He came to give us the truth that leads to abundant life. Thriving is Jesus' abundant life freely flowing through our lives.

When we agree with God about ourselves, we begin to believe truths like these:

- I am forever and continuously loved.
- I am fully pleasing to my Father.
- I am completely forgiven of my sins, past, present and future.
- I am totally accepted as his son or daughter.
- I have access to the riches of God's kingdom and I have an inheritance in him as his child.
- I don't have to fear the future, because God is with me, will watch over me and guide me into the good plans he has for me.

These truths are like fertilizer for our development as leaders. They anchor us in living truth and help us know we are loved and cared for. Coaching leaders are growing in the security of their identity and encourage others to grow in theirs. They give other leaders permission to be themselves and live from the life-giving reality of a loved son or daughter.

Deeper-level questions

1. Where would you say your identity is rooted?
2. Why is identity foundational to a life of flourishing in Christ?
3. How much agape (eternal, unbroken, sacrificial love) have you experienced in your life as a leader? Where and how did you experience it?
4. How much eros (selfish, conditional love) have you experienced in your life as a leader? Where and how did you experience it?
5. How often do lies (deceptive thoughts from the enemy that do not line up with the Word) trip you up and hinder your walk with God?

Potential action steps

1. Study the Scriptures and excellent books on the nature and character of God the Father.
2. Try to recognize when you are operating in orphan thinking and when you are operating in son/daughter thinking.
3. Practise saying out loud the truths in this chapter about your identity as a beloved son/daughter.

9. WE THRIVE WHEN WE COOPERATE WITH OUR GOD-GIVEN DESIGN

> For you created my inmost being;
> you knit me together in my mother's womb.
> I praise you because I am fearfully
> and wonderfully made;
> your works are wonderful,
> I know that full well.
>
> Psalm 139:13–14, NIV

Effortless

I love mornings. I was up early one April day on the south coast of England. I got up before breakfast to take a walk and enjoy the sea. The sound of a light breeze was mixed with the clamour of coastal birds singing their morning song. It sounded as if they were calling out to the new day.

I was due to preach in a few hours at a church in nearby Bournemouth, and I wanted to take some quiet time to pray and connect with God. I connect with God in the outdoors. I found a seat on a bench overlooking the cliffs and sat quietly, taking in the beautiful view before me. The sky was grey with clouds and a light mist was in the air. I zipped up my coat against the cold. Everything was still and peaceful.

Then I saw him.

A lone seagull was making his way along the beach about 20 ft above the cliffs, 50 ft off the water. A seagull at the beach is not all that remarkable. What got my attention was how he was flying: effortlessly.

He was gliding along with complete ease. His wings were fixed in the breeze: no flapping, no striving, no strain and no stress. He delicately adjusted his wings to the updraughts of air along the cliffs. He was barely moving, yet soaring above it all. The effortless ease of his peaceful progress was stunning and beautiful.

My soaring seagull friend is a gorgeous picture of what can happen when leaders begin to cooperate with their design. After we discover our true identity in Christ, our next step is to learn to cooperate with our God-given design. When we begin to do this, a supernatural ease and momentum emerges in our lives. As coaching leaders, we can help leaders learn to live from a place of rest that feels like effortless soaring. It doesn't come instantly or easily, but the potential to soar is real. It doesn't mean we don't have work to do, but it does mean our work takes on a new dimension. When we entrust our design to the Lord, wait on him and catch the wind of his Spirit, we can mount up with wings like an eagle.

Let's learn from Isaiah:

He gives strength to the weary,
And to *him who* lacks might He increases power.
Though youths grow weary and tired,
And vigorous young men stumble badly,
Yet those who wait for the LORD
Will gain new strength;
They will mount up *with* wings like eagles,

They will run and not get tired,

They will walk and not become weary.

(Isaiah 40:29–31, NASB)

There is divine power in knowing your design. There is increased strength in cooperating with how God made you. Each one of us is designed differently. We have different features and different abilities; different histories and different temperaments. We have different callings, but we have one clear thing in common: we were created on purpose. Our design tells us a lot about our purpose and how we can shine God's light to others. When we discover our design and how we naturally reflect Jesus, something inside us comes alive.

A seagull's body is designed for wind, water, air and sky. His wings are perfectly created to catch ocean air currents. Flight is his birthright. You don't have to explain to him who he is and what he was born to do. That is how design works. Our design reflects our purpose. God created him to fly, so he designed him for flight. Everything in his body aligns with the purpose God created him for. God built into him all the tools necessary to fly.

Picture a bottlenose dolphin gliding through the ocean at high speed. Her clicking and movement almost give the impression she's bursting with joy as she rockets up and down through the waves. She was created to swim, so God designed her with the body and energy to burst through the waves. Watching her, you are struck with a wonderful thought: 'That dolphin was born to swim.'

The examples of these creatures living from their design illustrate one of the foundational principles of thriving: *we find momentum when we cooperate with our God-given design.* Momentum releases freedom, fruit and fulfilment.

Let's look at each of these:

- *Freedom.* When we cooperate with our design, it feels as though we've been given permission to be ourselves. It is incredibly freeing to relax into how we are designed. We are no longer frustrated, trying to live someone else's life. We can be ourselves. We can rest and begin to do what we were born to do, just like a bird was born to fly.
- *Fruit.* We are able to do some things effortlessly – things that others struggle to do. God brings fruit through us like an apple tree bearing apples. It is not remarkable for an apple tree to make apples. It's what God designed it to do. The same is true for us. When we discover our design, we find that we bear certain kinds of fruit effortlessly. It gives God glory when we bear a ton of fruit.
- *Fulfilment.* There is something deeply satisfying about doing things you were born for. Fulfilment, being and doing what God created you for, is something every heart longs for. When you are living in alignment with your design, you sense God's pleasure over your life. You run and feel God smiling over you.

God built into you all the tools you need to fulfil your destiny. You were designed to do the works he created you for. Your role is to learn how you are designed and to work through the strengths and weaknesses of that design. In time, you will learn to live in alignment with God's purpose through your design. It's simple and yet it's profound. When we start to cooperate with the Creator's vision, design and purpose for our lives, a whole new reality unfolds for us.

Thriving in our design

As a leadership coach, I've seen many leaders who feel
stuck and frustrated in their work. They are not thriving.
They have spent years doing things they hate and are not
gifted to do. They don't feel alignment or momentum in
their destiny because they are not cooperating with their
design.

I've also seen leaders who discover the effortless joy of
living from their design. As they begin to cooperate with their
design, they feel like a bird set free from a cage. They learn to
align their time and efforts with their design. The result is an
explosion of joy, satisfaction and fruit. It is a fabulous thing
to watch.

Discovering your design is a process and takes effort, study
and trial and error. When we find our unique design and live
from it, we find a freedom that is truly remarkable. Let's dig
deeper into the power of design.

> For we are God's handiwork, created in Christ Jesus to do good
> works, which God prepared in advance for us to do.
> (Ephesians 2:10, NIV)

Discovering our design

Learning my design was a lot like learning how to fly. When
I discovered how God had designed me, I experienced a
freedom to be myself in ways I had never encountered before,
like a young eagle learning to fly. Finding my design set me
free to live and serve others with peace and joy.

As I uncovered how God had created me, it gave me
insight into how he wanted to use me. Understanding my
wiring meant I no longer struggled to know how to spend
my time. I stopped pouring tons of energy into things that

didn't align with my design. As much as possible, I eliminated from my schedule things that drained me and produced little fruit.

For years, I exhausted myself trying to implement the latest thing I'd read in a book or had heard at the most recent conference I'd attended. In all that effort, I knew something was missing. It was frustrating. I had not yet discovered my design. But once I started to get clarity in my design, it felt as though a divine wind began to rise up under my wings. God's favour and his Holy Spirit began to blow in the direction of my calling. I experienced a significant increase in joy and momentum in my work.

God moulds us and shapes us like clay on a potter's wheel. He fashions us into the masterpiece he has in mind. The scripture quoted from Ephesians says that we are God's workmanship. We are individual works of art created by a loving Artist. Our design shows the type of artwork we are to become.

Here are several things that come into focus when we learn our design:

- We come into rest, knowing who we are and what we were meant to do.
- We learn the way we naturally, effortlessly bear fruit.
- We find out the types of work that bring us the most joy and satisfaction.
- We discover the types of role that fit our design. This is a key step in learning to thrive.
- We get clarity on the areas that are not natural for us. By learning this we use our time more wisely.
- We have a helpful grid to evaluate how we spend our time. Thriving leaders spend most of their time living and leading from their strengths.

- We discover how our design best fits and cooperates with the design of others.
- We can delegate to others the tasks that fit naturally with their design and calling.

The process of cooperating with your design is something that never ends in a leader's life.

I've been introduced to several helpful tools through the years that help us in learning our design. These are a few I've experienced:

- Myers–Briggs Type Indicator
- DISC profile
- Enneagram
- Gallup Strengthsfinder 2.0
- PDP
- Colby
- Spiritual gifts tests.

I'm sure there are probably a dozen more helpful tools in this area. These assessments give us valuable information on how we are designed. As we process the results of each one, we begin to see the particular image God has placed within us. We start to get clarity in our design.

Early on in my journey following Jesus, I was introduced to a spiritual gifts test. I learned that I have God-given gifts of encouragement, teaching, leadership and sometimes prophecy. God designed me with those gifts and I was encouraged by my church to find ways to serve others with them. This was my introduction to the concept of God-given design.

I learned in these assessments that I am extroverted, intuitive in my decision making, value-driven and I love solid structure. I learned that I prefer to influence others with words of inspiration and my example rather than tell them what to do. I learned that I think and act fast; sometimes too fast. I learned that I love to work with others one to one and help them discover their gifts and potential.

As coaching leaders, we help leaders get clarity on their mix of gifts and strengths. Then we assist them to think through the areas where they can cooperate with their design. We help them to be honest with where they are not operating in their design too. When leaders begin to serve from their design, it's as though a light switch turns on. They are energized and excited about their work and their future.

As coaching leaders, we must anchor ourselves in this truth:

> We are not created to have all the gifts. We are only asked
> to steward our gifts for the good of others and the glory
> of God.

This truth is liberating. As we face the challenges of leadership, we are bombarded by a multitude of issues and needs. It is easy to feel that we need to be great at a million different things. In all honesty, there are some things we will never be great at. God did not design us to be great at them. When we embrace this truth, we can rest and let others come forward with gifts that complement our gifts. Their design nicely synergizes with our design. And when we work together in love and trust, a fuller picture of Jesus is revealed in our current situation.

Design is powerful. To get a biblical view of how design works, let's examine Romans 12:6–8.

> Having then gifts differing according to the grace that
> is given to us, *let us use them*: if prophecy, *let us prophesy*

in proportion to our faith; or ministry, *let us use it* in *our*
ministering; he who teaches, in teaching; he who exhorts,
in exhortation; he who gives, with liberality; he who leads,
with diligence; he who shows mercy, with cheerfulness.
(NKJV)

In these verses, the apostle Paul writes about a wonderful
variety of design that God has placed in his body. He has wired
all people uniquely and specifically in every culture on the
planet. No two people are alike. We are all different, but there
are patterns that can give us great insight and help us thrive.

Paul is reminding the church that there are seven different
giftings, or wirings, in the body of Christ. These are seven
predominant ways that people are designed by God. They are
key indicators of the motivations inside each person. As
coaching leaders, understanding leaders' design helps us grasp
why they do what they do and what God may be inviting
them to do. In my work with lots of leaders, knowledge of
these seven wirings has been extremely valuable in helping
them cooperate with their design and thrive.

This next list looks at the seven different wirings in the
body of Christ and their characteristics when they are at their
best:

- *Prophet.* Knows the mind of God. Sees the design of
  God. Sees God's perspective on everything before seeing
  man's perspective. Black and white. Very opinionated.
  Bold and dynamic in his or her faith. Examples: John
  the Baptist, Caleb, Elijah and Peter.
- *Servant.* Sees external needs and loves to meet them.
  Easily obeys God's directions. Good follower and
  can make a great leader. Cares about the comfort
  of others. Very little ambition. No need to be the

centre of attention. Examples: Esther, Barnabas, Timothy and Joseph (Mary's husband).

- *Teacher.* Values and needs to validate truth. Can reduce complex issues into core principles. Cares about accuracy, pure doctrine and correct thinking. Can bring out fresh bread from the Word to feed God's people. Safe emotionally. Not judgmental. Examples: Daniel, Luke, Levi, Samuel and Mordecai.
- *Exhorter.* Visionary. Wants to affect more people. Sees and shows God's extravagance. Energetic and exudes life wherever he or she is. Ministers the Word eloquently. Inspires and mobilizes God's people into the purposes of God. Examples: Moses, Paul and Jeremiah.
- *Giver.* Naturally understands money and stewardship. Versatile, flexible and independent. Excellent at birthing things. Knows how to build wealth. Excited to steward God's money for God's glory. Cares about future generations. Examples: Abraham, Jacob, Job and Matthew.
- *Ruler.* Natural leader, loves to be in charge of everything. Good administrator, thrives under pressure, skilled at time management. Can break down complex tasks into smaller component parts. A builder and governor for God. Examples: Joseph, Nehemiah, Solomon and Noah.
- *Mercy bringer.* Values worship and the beauty of God. Most sensitive of all the gifts. Senses the emotions of God's heart. Feels the emotions of others. Designed for intimacy. Easy access to the presence of God. Helps people feel safe and accepted. Examples: John the Beloved, Mary of Bethany, Ruth and David.

Jesus Christ lived out perfectly and lovingly all seven wirings at once. The Bible says that all the fullness of the godhead dwelt in him in bodily form. He was the complete package. God wants to grow us more and more into his image, but we will never be completely mature in all seven.

Picture God as the Master Artist. The seven design gifts are the primary colours that God uses to paint a picture of his nature across the earth. Each of the design gifts reveals a different aspect of the nature and goodness of God. There is an infinite variety of colour and expression that comes from these seven primary wiring colours. God reveals himself in all his amazing beauty and colour through his people. When these design gifts are redeemed and filled with the light of Christ, the glory and goodness of God are visible to the world.

If you don't know your design gift, you could spend years attempting to fulfil a destiny you were not created for. It's very frustrating and an epic waste of time. Finding your primary design gift and learning your strengths and weaknesses gives you a framework you can work from. You don't waste your energy working on things you were not designed for. Time becomes an investment as you sow your gift intentionally. Your efforts become more fruitful and enjoyable because you are cooperating with your design.

When you learn your design gift and study all the other gifts, it helps you relate to others with much more grace and understanding. You begin to see the underlying reasons for some of the differences and misunderstandings you experience in your relationships. People don't see things differently to annoy us or be in conflict with us. They see things differently because God designed them that way! There is strength, beauty and power in all the gifts working together in humility and unity. It is what the body of Christ was meant to do: reveal Christ in the earth.

Matching our time with our design

Tying together our design with the way we spend our time is explosive. I'll explain more of this later. In my coaching practice, when leaders learn their design and start to live from it, it's transformational.

Certain things bring you life and are enjoyable to you. Other things are very draining and life-stealing for you. We need to pay attention to these realities. It is not possible to spend 100% of our time on the things that bring us life. Real life doesn't work that way. Neither can we spend 100% of our time on things that we hate doing and steal life from us. That kind of life is unsustainable.

Living and leading from our design

Your gifts don't make you any more important or more loved by God. Your gifts were given to you by the grace of God. Your role is to steward those gifts. Like the parable of the talents in Scripture, God asks you to bring a return with the talents you have. You are called to invest those talents into the work of his kingdom. In reality, they are not your gifts, but his. He placed gifts inside us and knows how to bring them to their highest expression.

Deeper-level questions

1. How clear do you feel you are about your God-given design?
2. What assessments have you taken or material have you read to help you understand how God created you? If you've explored your design in these ways, what have you learned about how you are wired?
3. How much of your working time is spent cooperating with your design? Identify a percentage.

4. If you could do any type of work or ministry that cooperated with your design, what would it be?
5. If money were no obstacle, what type of work would you love to do full time for the rest of your life?

Potential action steps

1. Take a Gallup Strengthsfinder 2.0 assessment. When you purchase a new Strengthsfinder book, there is a code in the back. Take the online test and study which five strengths you have, then read in depth what they say about your wiring.
2. Study the seven motivational gifts of Romans 12:6–8. Try to identify which gift most aligns with your heart and behaviours.
3. Watch some YouTube videos or read up on the nine Enneagram personality types. Study until you discover how you are wired. Read and learn about the strengths and weaknesses of your type and whether they are true of you.
4. Do a time study to see what percentage of your work time is spent cooperating with your design.

10. EACH OF US HAS A SWEET SPOT: THE PLACE WE MOST NATURALLY BEAR FRUIT

Likewise, every good tree bears good fruit,
but a bad tree bears bad fruit. A good tree cannot
bear bad fruit, and a bad tree cannot bear good fruit.
Every tree that does not bear good fruit is cut down
and thrown into the fire. Thus, by their fruit
you will recognize them.

Matthew 7:17–20, NIV

Discovering a leader's sweet spot

The picture of flourishing in Psalm 92 is one of a healthy tree bearing much fruit. As coaching leaders, we want to help leaders discover and live from their sweet spot. The sweet spot is a key pathway to flourishing. Thriving, godly leaders bear fruit throughout their lifetime. Our sweet spot is the place where we naturally bear the most fruit for the kingdom.

It's exciting and beautiful to see leaders freed up to be themselves. Our sweet spot is like a vein where we consistently find gold. When miners discover a rich vein of gold in the earth, they follow that vein to get all the gold out of it. It's the same with us. Our sweet spot is a vein where our gold keeps showing up. It shows us patterns or certain ways God tends to use us and bear fruit through us. As coaching leaders, it's important we pay attention to the veins of gold we discover in people.

In our sweet spot, we carry an authority and a flow that is clear and consistent. Our sweet spot is predictable and familiar. There is a rest and a peace when we are there. We don't strive in our sweet spot; we just bear fruit and, when we are operating from it, we can't explain why we do those things so easily and naturally. The sweet spot is just a manifestation of God's grace to us.

Our sweet spot keeps coming up again and again as a place from which we can serve effectively in the kingdom. It's thrilling to know you are not a copy of someone else's design. It brings you great hope when you understand God made you specifically and uniquely to do certain things quite well.

One of the main reasons we feel stuck is that we are not cooperating with our design. We are doing things and living life with the wrong tools, like playing tennis with a golf club. The process of uncovering our design is like rubbing over a coin under paper with a pencil. Whatever is on the coin will be revealed through the paper as you rub the pencil over it. The image emerges and becomes clear.

Our unique design is something that emerges as we intentionally seek to understand it better. Every new discovery helps us know who we are and what we are uniquely designed to do. As we discover our unique design, we begin to feel an inner permission to be the person God created us to be. We are free to be ourselves. We stop trying to be good at everything, which is impossible. We let others do the things they do naturally and we do poorly. We find that some things bring us life and joy and others drain us terribly. When we narrow our focus to our unique design, our results improve and our stress level goes down. The longer we try to be good at everything, the more frustrated and fatigued we become.

When we live from our sweet spot, we begin to find an almost limitless supply of energy for our daily tasks we didn't know we had. We start loving the work we are doing. We find we are increasingly fruitful in our work. It's as if a burst of wind hits our sails and we launch off towards an exciting future.

Our unique design is made up of three main things:

1. *Our passion.* Where is the fire in your heart? What things do you absolutely *love* doing? You find you have extraordinary energy for these things. You feel incredibly alive and joyful when you are doing them. What issues light up your heart and mind with fierce passion and determination?

2. *Our wiring.* How did God uniquely create you? This is the unique design given to us by God. We are simply stewards of the gifts he's given us. We are wired to do some things extremely well. We do some things very naturally and effectively. Our design is a powerful indicator of the type of work the Father created us to do. We must pay attention to our unique design. We discover this through assessments and the motivational gifts in Romans 12:6–8.

3. *Our fruit.* This is key. Where do you see your life making the greatest impact for good with the least amount of effort? What do you do that people around you say is really helpful?

If we take the time and effort to deeply understand how we are wired, what we are passionate about and what we do naturally that helps others, we are discovering our sweet spot. It is not a quick or easy process. It takes effort, like mining for gold takes effort.

We all have to do things that are uncomfortable and hard for us. For those things we need discipline and intentionality. But we can also feel trapped in an environment where we are constantly asked to work outside our design. We dread each new day because we know we are going to spend most of our time doing tasks we hate. It can feel like punishment.

There is a better way. We can move beyond just existing and discover the place where we thrive. We can discover roles and tasks that feel incredibly natural for us. We can find that place of wonder and excitement called our sweet spot.

You are looking for the image of Christ that God has uniquely placed inside you. Your unique design gives you direction and guidance in your journey to thriving. It helps you organize your time around things that energize you and help others the most.

When I discovered this principle of unique design, I remember saying to myself, 'Spending most of my time doing the things I love, the things I am good at and the things that help others the most? Now that's something I can do!'

Figure 2 illustrates the three parts of our sweet spot and where they intersect. Let's look at each of these in more detail

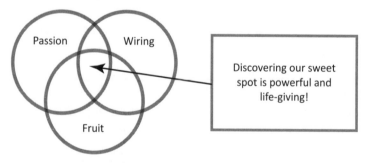

Figure 2: The sweet spot point of intersection

Our passion

My coach helped me identify the passions of my heart. Certain things bring up a fire in my spirit. When I think about them, my heart comes alive and I can feel God's passion burning inside me.

We were created with certain desires and longings that are easy to identify but hard to explain. We just know that when we think about certain needs or causes, we feel a divine energy pulsing through our veins. Vision and desire around those issues are not hard to access. Something deep inside tells us we were born to make a difference in those areas.

I believe passions like this are not just our own desires. I believe God put them there and he has a reason for them. The issues and causes that burn within us are signposts of the works God might be calling us into. The Holy Spirit seems to awaken us over time to specific good works that God has prepared for us to do. Our job is to listen to our passions and ask God, 'What are you calling me into in this?'

Psalm 37:4 says: 'Delight yourself in the LORD, and he will give you the desires of your heart' (ESV). This scripture can be interpreted in lots of ways, but in this context, I believe the meaning that is most helpful is that God places certain desires in our hearts that line up with his desires when we surrender those desires to him. Delighting in him is placing his desires and his will above our own.

Working in our areas of passion is a key to thriving. We feel a sense of joy and purpose bursting inside as we work on the issues most important to our hearts.

Coaches can help us discover our passions by asking key questions like:

- If money were no object, what issues or challenges would you tackle?

- What types of activities and projects give you life?
- Are there issues and tasks you enjoy so much, you lose all sense of time?
- What things would you stay up all night doing if you could?
- What types of work give you energy?
- When you are at rest and think about the world, what topics and issues repeatedly come to your mind?

Questions like these are signposts for our passions. As we align our working life with our passions, fresh bursts of joy and purpose rise up within us. We feel a satisfaction and renewed energy that propels us forward.

Our wiring

We have covered a significant part of our wiring in the chapter on our design. Here are a few more helpful thoughts.

Our wiring is like a set of divine fingerprints on our life. How we are made reveals the intention God had for us when he created us. Discovering our unique design is a holy and sacred thing. We must honour the gifts God has placed inside of us. We are stewards of those gifts.

Imagine a dolphin spending all her life working hard at flying. It sounds ridiculous. She could work herself to death and still not come into the sweet spot God created her for. It would be a tremendous waste of her God-given design. It would not honour the gifts he had given her.

Ultimately, you can only be yourself. God's divine fingerprints are all over your life. Take the time to discover what your gifts are and what they mean for you and your calling. Cooperate with them and you will begin to step into your sweet spot.

Our fruit

The area of our fruit is another key indicator of our sweet spot. Our fruit is the things we do naturally that help others the most. To us they seem like simple things everyone probably does easily. Others will tell us how we naturally help them. Ask them. Our fruit is what we do that brings life or adds value to those around us.

Discovering this fruit-bearing part of our sweet spot is invigorating. Our fruit comes directly from our unique design. We need to pay attention to it. We expect a peach tree to make peaches. That's not very remarkable. But if we look at this more deeply, it is the peach tree's role to do what it was designed to do: make peaches. Peach trees that work hard at trying to make pecans will be frustrated and bear no pecans. Your role is to bear the fruit you were designed to bear.

Fruit in the life of a leader works the same way. We are good at certain things. If you are good with details and numbers, budgets and accounting make sense to you. You have energy for looking at large stacks of data and finding what that data means. It's easy for you. You need to pay attention to this.

If you are good with people and easily connect with lots of different types of folks, you need to do things that involve people. People don't drain you, they give you energy. You don't have to work at it – it just happens for you. Find the areas of work and leadership that perfectly cooperate with your type of design and move towards those types of tasks.

I have worked with leaders who have never identified their sweet spot. They experience the opposite of thriving. Work is exhausting and joyless for them and they seem to bear little fruit. They feel they are chained to their work instead of liberated by it. Constantly tasked with working outside their sweet spot, they have frequent thoughts of quitting or escaping to do something they really want to do. There is a better way.

Let's dig deeper into how the sweet spot works. The sweet spot is the intersection of our passions, wiring and fruit (look again at Figure 2). It is where all three of those areas of our lives come together into one flow. It takes some discernment and prayer to identify it clearly. Coaching Leadership is a fantastic way to discover our sweet spot. With a caring leader walking alongside us, we can reach it more quickly.

The 80/20% principle

As I worked with my coach, Bob Logan, he shared with me an amazing concept: *thriving leaders spend 80% of their time working in their sweet spot.* They get to do what they do best most of the time. From this place of 80%, they feel liberated and experience a momentum that keeps building and multiplying. Work isn't painful or a bottomless pit. Work is the joy of getting to do what they were born and designed to do.

To get to 80% in our sweet spot takes tremendous focus and discipline. We have to form the ability to say 'no' to lesser things and 'yes' to the specific things we feel are in our sweet spot. We have to make many detailed decisions on what we will do with our time.

The key to thriving is letting go of tasks and responsibilities that are not in our sweet spot. In time, with helpful coaching, we can learn to delegate or eliminate things from our to-do list that are not in our sweet spot. Incredible freedom and fruit come when we learn to empower others in their own sweet spot. When you have a team of people living from this spot, bearing amazing fruit naturally, a picture of the body of Christ starts to beautifully unfold.

You cannot escape the 20% of things you don't enjoy. I call these the *challenge spot*. Life simply does not allow us to get away from this. Some things need to be done even if we are not the best at them. Being a responsible leader requires us to do and steward things that are not in our sweet spot. We have to learn the skills to manage these tasks as best we can.

Our goal is to increase our time in our sweet spot and decrease our time in the other tasks. Let's say you discover you are living 40% in your sweet spot and 60% in your challenge spot. Life is really an uphill climb because you're spending most of your working hours in things you struggle with.

If you know you are not in your sweet spot, it's time for some productive change. Ask yourself these questions:

- How can I free up time to increase my percentage in my sweet spot?
- What things can I pass along to others who are naturally good in that area?
- What types of things have I kept doing simply because I thought that was what was needed from me?
- What would happen if I gave myself permission to make a change and move towards my sweet spot?

In time, you'll discover there are some simple, practical next steps you can take to move towards your sweet spot. I've seen many leaders do this successfully. Each step towards their sweet spot brings a burst of joy and energy. Every release of things in their challenge spot feels like a heavy weight being lifted off their shoulders.

The 80/20% principle is a wonderful mental framework from which to think about thriving. God created us to thrive and do the things we were designed to do. Most leaders have never entered a disciplined process to shift these percentages and free themselves for their best work.

Coaching is incredibly helpful at this point. When I begin to coach new leaders, I ask them to share with me the results from several personality and gifts tests. After reviewing these, I spend time asking them lots of deeper questions around their passions, wiring and fruit. In time, their sweet spot emerges organically. I can see it and so can they. For most, it is an exhilarating process.

A key part of coming into our sweet spot is realizing we have the power to make changes that lead to thriving. We are not victims in this life. As we get clarity around our sweet spot, decisions about what we do and how we spend our time also become clear.

Even if your boss or team members are screaming at you to handle certain things, you can calmly and confidently say 'no' and help the team find the right person for that task. Look for another person who has a sweet spot in that area. If there is truly no-one else to handle it, you can do the task as a part of your 20%. Just don't allow others to handcuff you to your challenge spot. As you pray, think and decide on your future, you need to be constantly aware of your sweet spot and trying to grow that percentage up to 80% in your working life.

Thriving in our sweet spot

You come alive in your sweet spot. It will always feel like a gift to you rather than a drain on you. We must learn to say 'yes' to it more and more, and delegate or say 'no' to things that don't fall within it. Gold shines brightly from this place because it is the way God made us to most naturally bear fruit. Get to know your sweet spot: study it, pray for it and spend time in it. As you do, God will be glorified and you will find joy.

Deeper-level questions

1. What would be your greatest passion in the area of your work/ministry?
2. Do you feel that you are operating most of the time from your sweet spot?
3. What makes the sweet spot so empowering and energizing?
4. What are the things you feel you must do to answer God's call on your life? Where are you spending more time: in the 'can do' box or in the 'must do' box?
5. What fruit do you feel you bear naturally in the work of the kingdom with little effort?

Potential action steps

1. Identify your sweet spot and write it down so you can look at it.
2. Say 'no' to one thing you're doing this week that is not even remotely close to your sweet spot, so you will have more time to operate from your sweet spot.
3. Delegate something that is not in your sweet spot to someone who has theirs in that area.

11. THE CROSS: GOD'S GREAT REFINING TOOL

For Christ did not send me to baptize, but to preach
the gospel, not with wisdom of words, lest the
cross of Christ should be made of no effect.
For the message of the cross is foolishness
to those who are perishing, but to us who
are being saved it is the power of God.

1 Corinthians 1:17–18, NKJV

The heat of refining

In the lifelong process of refining godly leaders, the cross of
Christ is the pre-eminent instrument of transformation.
God's refining processes are always designed to bring us life,
but they don't always feel that way. The cross, on which Jesus
suffered and died, is not a pretty thing, but it is a powerful
life-giving tool in the hands of God. For the Christian leader,
death is the pathway to life and freedom. In the kingdom of
God, death has no victory and no sting. Death is not something to fear. When we leave this body, we are released to an
eternity in the presence of God. As Christian leaders, when
we experience death to our self-life, our pride and our rights,
the resurrection life of Christ brings us joy, hope and peace.
The cross is where we die so we can live.

Praise be to God, the cross was not the end of the story for Christ and, when we embrace it as leaders, it is not the end for us either. The cross was the hinge point of the gospel, because the death of Jesus paid the penalty for our sins and opened the floodgates for the resurrection life of God to fill the hearts of us all. For us who are being saved and transformed by Christ, the cross is the power of God.

When my first church plant ended and we closed the church, I had some deep soul-searching to do. I had to face some parts of myself that were ugly and selfish. I had to own some sinful ways that had hurt others. I had to go to certain people and repent of my sins and offences towards them. It was a difficult and crushing process for my ego and my confidence. It was a personal encounter with the cross.

As I came through that experience of death and repentance, an amazing thing began to happen. Death released new life within me that was incredible. I experienced a freedom to be myself, let go and trust God. I found myself loving others more freely and consistently than ever before. I experienced the transforming power of the cross and the gospel and it set me free. I experienced, with Christ, the power of his resurrection. My prayer, along with Paul, became:

> that I may know him and the power of his resurrection,
> and may share his sufferings, becoming like him in his death,
> that by any means possible I may attain the resurrection
> from the dead.
> (Philippians 3:10–11, ESV)

Allowing the cross to have its way in me led me down the road to flourishing. The cross is God's great refining tool, which helps us identify with Jesus in his death so we may be like him in his resurrection. We must embrace the cross.

As Christian leaders, we can experience a supernatural life, where we are no longer living and leading, but Christ himself is living through us. This is what Paul meant when he said:

> I have been crucified with Christ. It is no longer I who live, but Christ who lives in me. And the life I now live in the flesh I live by faith in the Son of God, who loved me and gave himself for me.
> (Galatians 2:20, ESV)

Helping others embrace the cross

As coaching leaders, we are allowed the privilege of close access to the lives and hearts of the leaders we serve. In strong coaching relationships, we build trust, which allows us to walk closely with leaders in their darkest hours. From this precious space, we can partner with the Holy Spirit as he leads a leader from death to life. We can be instruments that help leaders move into the fullness of what God created them for. This is the power of Coaching Leadership and the cross of Christ.

As Christian leaders, death to self is not always our first choice. The cross is painful and the flames of refining are excruciatingly hot. This is God's method of purifying gold. God uses it all – the nails, the piercing of our side and the crown of thorns – in our refining process. Both Peter and Paul faced their own crosses and so will we. The cross is a critical part of our growth and maturity as leaders.

As is so often true in the kingdom, God uses an unlikely and opposite dynamic to bring us into life: we are emptied to be filled, humbled so he can exalt us and we give first before we receive. This is what happens when we embrace the cross of Christ. We die and then we live.

The redemptive value of pain

When we experience the cross, God is very present with us in our pain. Paul lived out this reality. He is one of the most thriving, fruitful leaders in history. We are still reading Paul's words now and studying his incredible revelation about Jesus and the gospel. He still influences us to this day. He stands as a giant in the list of Christian leaders.

If you were to ask Paul what was the greatest instrument God used to shape him as a leader, he would say one thing: the cross. He would declare that the cross was God's great refining tool.

In 2 Corinthians 12:9–10, Paul makes this statement:

> But he said to me, 'My grace is sufficient for you, for my power is made perfect in weakness.' Therefore I will boast all the more gladly about my weaknesses, so that Christ's power may rest on me. That is why, for Christ's sake, I delight in weaknesses, in insults, in hardships, in persecutions, in difficulties. For when I am weak, then I am strong.
> (NIV)

Paul's greatest fruit as a leader did not come from planting churches or preaching great sermons. His greatest contribution to the church and the world was his writing. Forced to be alone for five years in a Roman prison, Paul put down into words the theologies and the encouragements that have made an impact on billions of people throughout history.

Peter, who understood the cross personally and deeply, knew God was doing something through trials and pain. He wrote:

> In all this you greatly rejoice, though now for a little while you may have had to suffer grief in all kinds of trials. These have

come so that the proven genuineness of your faith – of greater
worth than gold, which perishes even though refined by fire –
may result in praise, glory and honour when Jesus Christ is
revealed. Though you have not seen him, you love him; and
even though you do not see him now, you believe in him
and are filled with an inexpressible and glorious joy, for
you are receiving the end result of your faith, the salvation
of your souls.

(1 Peter 1:6–9, NIV)

Refining and trials are meant to strengthen and purify our
faith, which Peter says is more precious than gold. Faith is the
doorway to things we hope for. We access the greater things
of the gospel and the kingdom by faith. God repeatedly tells
us in the Word, 'Trust me. Don't be afraid. If you have just a
little faith, I can do the impossible.' God's ultimate goal
through trials is to save our souls and bring us into joy
inexpressible and the fullness of his glory.

God uses pain and problems to grow us, purify us and
conform us into the image of Jesus. The death of a loved one,
betrayal by a close friend or a ministry collapse are all terribly
painful. But in the hands of a loving God, they can all be
transformed through the cross into life and hope and peace.
This is the miracle of the cross of Christ.

In these times, three anchor truths can sustain us in the
heat of our refining and keep us from despair and hopelessness.
We must hang on to the truths that God is:

1. *Present.* In our deepest pain, we must cling to the truth
   that God will never leave us. This is what he has
   promised. He is with us in our darkest days. He suffered
   himself and he draws near to us when we share in his
   sufferings. In our greatest pain, he is often the nearest

and tenderest to us, ready to help us and walk with us into life again.

2. *Sovereign.* Whatever difficult circumstance we have endured, God knows where we are and has allowed us to be there. This is a challenging truth that can set us free. Our pain is not random. God did not leave us and he is not trifling with us. He knows every detail of every difficult circumstance that comes into our lives. He knows the past, present and future, and will use that painful place to mould us and shape us for his future purposes. God knows where we are and he is with us.

3. *Good.* No matter how awful the trial, we must drive a stake in the ground and cling to the truth that God is good. In maritime stories, I've read of sailors who would lash themselves to the mast of a sailing ship during a terrible storm so they wouldn't be blown into the sea. It is similar with the truth of God's goodness. Bind yourself to this truth. Regardless of how circumstances and your feelings may scream at you, cling to the reality of God's goodness. In time, if you trust him with everything, he will reveal his redeeming goodness through the most horrible events of your life.

Warning lights

For several years I worked for General Electric, leading a complex manufacturing team. In that environment, we had to have strict manufacturing processes that depended on machines with tight tolerances. Those machines were engineered with warning lights that came on when a part was out of tolerance and an operator needed to stop the process. All our employees were trained to stop the manufacturing process when a warning light came on, so maintenance personnel could examine the machine and get it fixed. The concept of warning lights is critical as we look at God's refining process.

In God's refining process, there are warning lights that can help us deal with places inside us that may need to be brought to the cross. As coaching leaders, we need to pay attention to these warning lights and help leaders respond wisely for their growth and maturity. Warning lights are God's gift to us to show us where something is wrong and where we need some help.

Let's look at a few warning lights we need to pay attention to in ourselves and others that may point to a need for us to embrace the cross:

1. *Elevated stress and conflict with our spouse or in key relationships.* Life has normal ups and downs, but when we are experiencing significant and consistent conflict, we need to stop and find out what is happening in our primary relationships.
2. *Numbness in our hearts.* When we stop feeling or stop caring about life, our work or others, something is very wrong. We need to dig deep to find out why.
3. *Jealousy or resentment.* Sometimes our flesh kicks up and we resent that someone else is being blessed and we are not. We secretly get upset and angry that good things are happening to others but not to us. This is a danger sign. Pay attention. Search for a deeper understanding of what is driving those negative feelings and seek healing.
4. *Debilitating fatigue.* We all get tired, but there is a fatigue that is deep and dangerous. A good night of sleep won't cure this type of fatigue. We are closing in on burnout. If we ignore this warning light, a collapse or breakdown is very possible.

5. *Extreme emotions.* Severe bouts of anger are a sign that something needs attention in our emotional life. When we feel we want to quit and do something extreme, it's time to slow down and ask why. Maybe we need a real holiday or some time with a good counsellor, processing our motives. Extreme emotions are a big warning light. If we ignore this sign, we may find ourselves doing something dangerous to ourselves and others. Affairs and emotional breakdowns can result from a heart that feels trapped and is suffocating in pain. Both of these come at a horrible price. Get the help you need.

6. *Depressive or suicidal thoughts.* Depression is a real and common part of our world as leaders. It is often kept hidden because we fear others' judgment or misunderstanding. We don't want to appear weak or mentally unstable. This light needs immediate attention from people who are equipped to help us through it. There is professional medical help available and there are understanding people who will love us and not judge us. Find them.

7. *Relationship breakdown.* When we are seeing many of our relationships fall apart, we need to slow down and ask why. God may have us in a transition to a new place or a new role. But he may also want us to look at our hearts and ask how we may be contributing to the breakdown.

8. *Addictive behaviour.* Whenever we see addiction taking root in our lives, we need to stop and ask why. From pornography to alcohol or even films and entertainment, these things can become a substitute for relationship with God and those closest to us. When we use addiction to cope with life's stress, we need to find out what is driving our addictive behaviour and get the help and healing that will set us free.

9. *Thoughts of quitting/escape.* When we feel like giving up, we need to dig down and find out what is driving those feelings. All of us feel like throwing in the towel at times. When we become obsessed with thoughts of escape, we need a change of some kind. Find some help to process your thoughts and emotions.

Warning lights are God's gift to us. Pain is not our enemy; it is a warning light. It can protect us from something more damaging that can happen if we don't make key changes. God uses pain in our lives to show us more deeply our need for him and how fragile life can be.

Breaking through into life

Several harmful patterns can keep us stuck and unable to break through into life. These patterns work against us, so we avoid the deep work of examining our hearts and embracing the cross. Therefore we never break through into resurrection life.

Let's look at them briefly.

1. *Distraction.* Busy lives can make us feel important. Surely someone as busy as we are must be doing significant, fruitful work, right? Not necessarily. Busyness can keep us distracted with less important things and from doing the deep work needed to get to our greatest contribution.
2. *Denial.* For some of us, ignoring real problems feels easier than facing our pain. We create elaborate ways to justify or explain away real issues we are facing. Denial is dangerous when we avoid problems that one day can become catastrophic. We need to deal with

issues when they are small and easily solved. Denial can allow issues to grow so big that we are in for a major crisis. Face them.

3. *Blame.* This is a subtle form of denial. We tell ourselves that other people or other issues are the cause of the things we are reaping. We find reasons why we could not be responsible for the problems we are experiencing. This harmful habit keeps us in victim mode and prevents us from owning the issue and growing beyond it. Blame also breaks the trust of our team members. Leaders need to honestly own their own problems and model a lifestyle of personal responsibility.

4. *Comfort zones.* Our comfort zones can become so safe and secure, we fight to defend them. But when we refuse to be disturbed in our places of comfort, it not only affects our own growth but the growth of our organization. Remaining undisturbed is dangerous when a true crisis is brewing in front of us. Facing the crisis and helping the team develop and grow past the problem is the goal. It can lead to breakthroughs that are breathtaking.

Healthy coaching can break through all these self-inflicted issues. Coaching leaders help you look honestly at your life, while supporting you as you walk through the valley of your dying process. Breaking blind spots and moving past your denial leads to real transformation in your life and leadership. Coaching leaders hold you accountable. They want you to get to where you feel God is leading you next.

> Every coaching session should result in one to three simple but effective next steps for your growth.

Your coach will revisit these action steps with you at your next session. That accountability alone leads to great motivation and change. Most of us will do the things we know others are holding us accountable for. This leads to breakthrough after breakthrough. Even small steps that are strategic and timely can lead to big breakthrough.

Other resources for our freedom

There is an increasing array of people and resources to help us look at our inner life; to assist us in coming through our pain and into freedom. Spiritual directors, counsellors, healing ministries, memorizing Scripture, and addiction programmes are well positioned to help us work through the pain and challenges of our growth and healing process. Reach out for these resources. Each of them has a different function and flow, but all are critical for particular issues and needs.

Pay attention to the seasons

Coaching leaders pay attention to the seasons that all leaders go through. It helps us cooperate with what the Holy Spirit is doing in a leader's life. These seasons may not always happen in sequence, but sometimes they do, just like in the natural world. Coaching leaders help leaders identify the season they are in. You cannot fight the season you are in spiritually any more than you can fight the natural seasons. You won't win. We help leaders embrace the season God has them in and discover how they can cooperate with the Father in that season.

Here's a look at the spiritual seasons we may find ourselves in:

1. *Summer:* a time of growth and blessing. Living feels easy and life is flowing freely.

2. *Autumn*: seems as if things are beginning to end.
   Something needs to change. Harvest comes from past
   sowing. Things are not growing as much.
3. *Winter*: hard times hit. Relationships can be strained
   or may end, sometimes painfully. It's cold and difficult.
   Death is hitting us hard. This is the place of the cross.
4. *Spring*: new life begins. Flowers and warmth return.
   Your heart finds its song again and leaves become fresh
   and green once more.

Have the same attitude as Jesus

Keep your eyes on Jesus throughout the process of refining.
He is the Author and Finisher of our faith. He knows how to
bring you through to flourishing. Remember the Scriptures'
encouragement to:

> run with endurance the race that is set before us, looking
> unto Jesus, the author and finisher of *our* faith, who for the
> joy that was set before Him endured the cross, despising
> the shame, and has sat down at the right hand of the throne
> of God.
> (Hebrews 12:1–2, NKJV)

Take on the same attitude as Christ (Philippians 2:1–8). Jesus,
though he was God's Son, chose death in obedience to his
Father. Because he willingly chose death, he came into the
fullness of all God wanted for him. Because he surrendered
all that he was, God used his life to the fullest to redeem all
mankind. Because he willingly chose the cross, Jesus was
given a name that is above every name. We must also choose
the cross. Death is the path to fullness, the door to abundance
and the highway to thriving.

Don't run from the high heat of the cross. Stay in the crucible when you are in the furnace of God's refining processes. Pay attention to the warning lights that are telling you something is wrong. God will meet you there and he will bring about his good plans for you.

Deeper-level questions

1. In what area might God be calling you to die to yourself so he can fill you with his resurrection life?
2. When you think of the cross of Christ, what is the first thing that comes to your mind? What does your answer tell you about your view of the cross?
3. What warning lights from this chapter have you seen show up in your own life in the past year?
4. What season of life (summer, autumn, winter or spring) are you in spiritually at this time in your journey with Christ?
5. Who in your life would be honest with you if you were operating in blame, denial or a victim mindset? If you have a name, have you given that person permission to speak truth to you in this area?
6. What is God potentially removing from your life through his refining processes?

Potential action steps

1. Ask the Holy Spirit to show you any area of your life where you are unwilling to die and take up your cross.
2. Take time to assess what season you are in right now (summer, autumn, winter, spring).
3. Be honest regarding your pain and tell God exactly how you feel about his refining processes in your life.

12. ALL TRUE THRIVING IS RELATIONAL

Abide in Me, and I in you. As the branch cannot
bear fruit of itself, unless it abides in the vine,
neither can you, unless you abide in Me.
I am the vine, you *are* the branches.
He who abides in Me, and I in him, bears
much fruit; for without Me you can do nothing.

John 15:4–5, NKJV

In my backyard I have four grape vines. On the October day we moved into our house, I found the vines had been neglected for several years and looked rather unkempt. I had no idea whether they would produce much fruit. Excited to have my own mini vineyard, I researched the best way to get a huge crop of delicious grapes. I found the key was pruning. To get the most delicious and the highest number of grapes, I had to cut back those four vines and cut them hard. I got out my clippers and started cutting. I cut them back so much they looked sad and barren. That's what the online gardener folks said to do.

The next spring, those vines came alive. Shoots started running everywhere. Then the grapes came. Man, did they come! It was unlike anything I had ever seen. Hundreds and hundreds of plump, juicy Concord grapes formed on those four simple vines that had looked bare and sickly eight months before. My whole family had a blast picking those delicious grapes, eating them and processing them into grape jelly.

Relationship is primary

John 15 gives us four critical lessons about how God views our relationship with him and our relationships with others. As coaching leaders, we must dig deep into these biblical truths. Jesus wants us to understand that:

- *God is the Gardener.* God relates to each of us as an attentive Father, eager and ready to help us thrive and bear fruit. He cares for his vines as though they are his children.
- *Pruning works.* God relates to us intentionally so we will bear more fruit. Pruning is a process that at first looks harsh and intimidating. Sometimes God relates with us in ways that appear, and feel, cruel and severe. That sounds like the refining of gold we have explored throughout this book. Despite the pain, pruning is always for our good.
- *The life is in the vine.* God shares his life freely with us. This is the biggest lesson of all and the focus of this chapter. Jesus has life for every leader in the world. His life changes everything.
- *Life without relationship is fruitless.* God says our relationship with him is primary. We are unable to thrive unless this relationship is vital and energized by the Spirit.

Thriving relationships are all about value. God values us, so he relates to us with great love. God sees you as a masterpiece and relates to you with great care and intentionality. If you had a work of art worth millions of dollars, you would relate to that artwork in a certain way. If your child drew you a personal picture saying how much he or she loved you, you would relate to that artwork in a way that reflected your relationship with the artist. You would love that artwork because you love the child.

Coaching Leadership is a life of loving relationship. To be a Christian leader is to relate to others in a particular way. We don't use people to pursue a goal; we love people as God is working his goals in them. Coaching Leadership requires humility and tenderness in our relationships. It calls for us to die to our personal ambitions so we can selflessly serve and build up others.

Paul's encouragement for relationships

Paul paints a picture of relational love and unity in Romans 12 that is worthy of our attention. Here is his encouragement to the disciples in Rome:

> Let love be genuine. Abhor what is evil; hold fast to what is good. Love one another with brotherly affection. Outdo one another in showing honor . . . Bless those who persecute you; bless and do not curse them. Rejoice with those who rejoice, weep with those who weep. Live in harmony with one another. Do not be haughty, but associate with the lowly. Never be wise in your own sight. Repay no one evil for evil, but give thought to do what is honorable in the sight of all. If possible, so far as it depends on you, live peaceably with all. (Romans 12:9–18, ESV)

Pay attention to the rich relational language here: genuineness, goodness, affection, honour, joy, blessing, compassion, harmony, humility and peace. This is the biblical picture of relational life. The atmosphere of Coaching Leadership flows with this kind of relational life. Paul's words drip with the beauty of heaven, a place where there is perfect harmony, relational unity and immense love. His words describe a community drawing life from Christ himself. Coaching leaders pursue this kind of relational reality.

Paul spends eleven chapters in Romans outlining the power and truth within the gospel of grace. Then in chapter 12, he describes what that gospel will do: transform our relationships so they are channels of the life and love of Jesus. The gospel heals and elevates our relationships to a level no human effort could ever achieve. As coaching leaders, we pay attention to the quality of our relationships because these are the greatest indicator of true thriving.

Boundaries are the key to thriving relationships

One of the keys to thriving in our relationships is to live within the limits of healthy boundaries. Many people have never thought about or heard anyone teach on the critical relationship between thriving and healthy boundaries. Boundaries are God's gift to us, not annoying handcuffs designed to limit our fun or our success. Boundaries are the atmosphere of love and the context in which real relational thriving can take place. Let me explain.

The Bible gives us freedom within healthy limits. The first example is when God told Adam and Eve they could eat from any tree of the garden, but not from the tree of the knowledge of good and evil. That one was off limits. We know the horrible result when they violated that boundary.

If we live beyond God's boundaries, we will miss the biblical thriving God created us for. As we coach leaders, we must help them process the relational aspects of their lives, not just their work and accomplishments. We must help them deal with boundary issues that are harming their relationships. An example would be a husband or wife who is pouring too much time and effort into being a success at work while neglecting relationship with their spouse and children. Thriving is a relational and work balance. It is a delicate balance. Leaders' emotional and relational health is at the core of their sense of thriving. When we violate healthy boundaries, our relationships always suffer; both with God and with those closest to us.

Learning your yeses and your noes

Healthy boundaries are the building blocks of a thriving life. If I could teach one required class to every person in the world, it would be a thorough course on boundaries. Boundaries help us build a life of order, peace and purpose. Without good boundaries, we never come into the fullness of what God created us for.

Good boundaries cooperate with the way the world works. A person with good boundaries is living in reality and knows that ultimately everything in life has an element of sowing and reaping. Boundaries teach us that if we do one thing, it has consequences and results. If we do something else, it has different consequences and results. People with good boundaries know where their time is going and can adjust things as they desire to get better results. Learning boundaries was a process for me.

For years I had terrible boundaries or no boundaries at all. My time was being wasted all over the place. I didn't know any better, but it just felt awful. The urgent elephant of time was dragging me here, there and everywhere and I felt like a victim. Time was my master; I was not the master of it. My family often got only the scraps of my best time and energy because I was pouring myself out on things that really didn't matter.

Once I discovered good boundaries, I began to learn to master my time. I discovered I am not a victim of time and do not have to live by the tyranny of urgent things. When things came up that were not helpful, I began to make changes and adjust my schedule. I learned to invest my time because I began to know what I wanted to accomplish. I paid attention to wasteful time stealers and began to eliminate those from my timetable. Boundaries played an especially critical role in learning to live from my sweet spot.

Learning boundaries helped me develop a strong, personal voice. I knew where I was going and what I was willing to do to get there. I formed the ability to say 'yes' and 'no' at the right times to the right things. Trivial things were told 'no' or delegated to someone who could do them more efficiently. Urgent but unimportant things were told 'no' and eliminated from my weekly routine.

Important but non-urgent tasks, on the other hand, were told 'yes' and regularly made it on to my calendar. I started to do important, strategic things that moved me towards my vision and goals. I began to taste the sweet fruit of momentum; to gain mastery over my time. I started telling the elephant of time what to do and to use my time to my advantage.

To thrive relationally, you must learn and understand the relational laws of boundaries. Coaching leaders are excellent thinking partners around the topic of boundaries.

Drink deeply yourself

One of my greatest mistakes through my life has been to focus too much on helping others, without doing the things I needed for my own nourishment and growth. When you fly commercially, the flight attendant will tell you that, in the event of an emergency, air masks will descend from above. You are to place the mask over your face and tighten the straps. The attendant also states: 'Put your mask on before helping others with their mask.'

This is a powerful principle: to take care of your own need for oxygen before you try to help others get theirs. If you are not breathing, you are not capable of helping anyone else. In coaching lots of leaders, I find this same dynamic to be common. I've seen leaders working so hard to help others grow and thrive, they have lost the ability to thrive themselves. I have encouraged them to regularly stop and breathe the oxygen of God's love for themselves, so that they have the health and strength to pour into others.

It is sad to see eager servant leaders working themselves into the ground, trying to get oxygen to people who are out of air when they are in critical need of oxygen themselves. It's like a person at an oasis in the desert who is standing by a spring of fresh, clear, cool water. Thirsty travellers come out from the desert to refresh themselves by that living water. Let's say that person focuses all his or her energy on helping others get a small cup of water, consumed with thinking about cups, distribution systems, water flow rates and a million other details.

The tragic truth is that person is standing right next to the source of living water, but is dying of thirst through being focused on the wrong thing: on helping everyone else without taking the time to drink that delicious water personally.

The better plan is to drink deeply of that living water. Let yourself be refreshed and filled up by it. Then start telling everyone who comes along how they can go to the wellspring and get refreshing water for themselves. This is God's desire for each of us. Focus on the source of living water first. Focus on the primary element of your relationship with Jesus. Abide in him. Come to the oasis and drink deeply of his life-giving water and presence. Allow God to fill you with his life. Then turn to others and invite them to drink with you. You don't have to pour it down their throats. When they see the joy and the fullness you are filled with, they will want to drink for themselves.

Cooperate with God's refining process in your life. He is always working to conform you into the image of Jesus. Drink deeply of the living water flowing from Jesus. Let his life become a well of life within you. Then point others towards him and his refreshing Holy Spirit. That is how thriving was meant to flow.

Our greatest investment

Our relationships are our place of greatest investment. If you relate to one person with the love of Christ for a lifetime, your life has been invested for eternity. People matter to God. They are the investment that will never lose value. Whether you are introverted or extroverted, relationships are still primary. Some of us will relate to thousands; others will relate to only a handful. The number of relationships we have is not important. What matters is the quality and purity of those relationships. If we love a few with the love of Christ in faith, humility and sincerity, we have invested our lives wisely.

Our relationships are infinitely more valuable than money. Jesus taught us that where our treasure is, there our heart will be also. Invest in your own development and in the development of other leaders. Jesus told us a parable about investing our talents to bring a return (Matthew 25:14–29). This kind of investing pleases the Master. Bringing people into the fullness of their calling is an eternal investment. Barnabas invested a significant part of his life into mining for the gold in the apostle Paul. He saw his relationship with Paul as a worthy investment of his best energy. The results changed the world. This is the beauty of Coaching Leadership. We devote our best relational energy into the development of godly leaders.

A wave of leadership development

I once attended a leadership development course at GE's corporate executive training centre in Crotonville, New York. I was a junior executive in the company and a bit wide-eyed with all the money and power around me in that place. One memory from there still speaks to me to this day. I was standing overlooking the Hudson River and enjoying some conversation with my fellow leaders, when the helicopter of GE's then chairman, Jack Welch, flew into the complex and landed on a heliport in the centre of the campus. As he exited the aircraft, an attendant handed him a Diet Coke, his favourite drink, and escorted him into a room full of GE's top executives, who were there for training. He was with them less than an hour and then hopped back on to his helicopter and headed off to GE headquarters. We all stood there amazed at the picture in front of us. GE was investing an incredible amount of time, energy and money into the development of its corporate leadership.

As I turned back to look at the river, I felt a strong sense of the Holy Spirit come over me. My heart cried out, more like a sigh, and I said this to the Lord: 'Lord, if the business world invests this much to develop leaders for the purpose of making money, how much more should we invest everything we have into the leaders who do your kingdom work all over the world!' My heart was burning with passion as I said it. I knew that picture was something I was to give my life to. Since that day I have prayed for God to raise up leaders who reflect Jesus and make an impact on the world for his kingdom. I have devoted my limited resources into developing one leader at a time. I believe the development of godly, thriving leaders is worth the investment of our best time, effort and resources.

I dream of a movement of leadership development, like a huge wave of the Spirit, which helps millions of leaders in every culture of the globe come into the fullness of what God has created them for. It is an investment of immense proportions. That one investment would change the face of the church, transform cities and heal nations. A huge investment into the work of helping godly leaders thrive would have a domino effect, touching life after life with the love and goodness of God. Picture in your mind millions of thriving Christian leaders. This is the vision I have for Coaching Leadership.

Your heavenly bank account will not be measured by material wealth or the trophies of accomplishments. It will be measured by the quality of your relationships, the care and commitment you shared with loved ones and the contribution you made into the lives of others. All of that is about relationships. Coaching Leadership is a relational paradigm. It functions and flows from healthy relationships.

Deeper-level questions

1. How would you describe the quality of your primary relationships (spouse, children, parents, siblings, close friends) at this time in your life?
2. What patterns of relationship health, or lack of it, do you see in your life?

3. How would you describe the quality and closeness of your relationship with Christ himself? God, the Father? The Holy Spirit?

4. How healthy are your boundaries in your primary relationships? How strong is your ability to say 'yes' and 'no' to the right things without guilt or shame?

5. How frequently do you take time to drink deeply of God's nourishment through the Word and the Spirit? Would you say your heart is dry, empty and broken? Or refreshed, watered and thriving?

Potential action steps

1. Do an inventory of your primary relationships and write down beside each person how strong and healthy your relationship is with them.

2. Look at your upcoming calendar to schedule some time away alone with God to seek his face, rest and listen for his voice over your life.

3. Write down how much time you have in your schedule for pouring into others versus how much time you have available for getting poured into by God. Reschedule some time with God so you have a healthy balance.

EPILOGUE:
NEXT STEPS TO THRIVING

Thriving is not just a good idea. It is your birthright (John 10:10). As a Christian leader, you were created by God to flourish and bring pleasant offerings for his glory (Psalm 92). In this Epilogue, let's turn our attention to next steps and answer the question: so what do I do now?

Look again to our definition of biblical thriving. Our goal in Mining for Gold is to develop godly, thriving leaders. Thriving leaders are:

1. *Flourishing.* They are growing and developing vigorously.
2. *Planted in community.* They put down roots and build deep and lasting relationships.
3. *Doing God's work.* They commit themselves to seeking his kingdom and his righteousness first.
4. *Bearing fruit.* They are living from their design and thriving from their sweet spot.
5. *Being continually renewed.* They are experiencing freshness and renewal regularly.

As coaching leaders, we want to help leaders experience this fullness. If you want help preparing for a marathon, competing in a crossfit competition or doing a triathalon, you hire a personal trainer. You will gladly pay a trainer if you feel he or she will encourage and stretch you towards accomplishing your goal. A physical trainer is there not to be your buddy, but to stretch you and help you get to places you cannot reach on your own. This is what Coaching Leadership is like. The coaching leader loves you and is willing to stretch you as you grow because he or she loves you.

The key to growth is simple: focus. When you focus on the right things, you move forward and develop. When you focus on the wrong things, you go backwards or stay stuck. Instead of focusing on many things, you need to focus on a few critical things to get to thriving. Let me share a story on the importance of correct focus.

Losing focus

'Let's go to work, men,' my commander shouted above the buzzing of the command tent. The flight briefing was over and we all headed out into a cold February night in Texas. It was time to fly.

The year was 1991 and America was at war. On 15 January, President Bush announced that the USA had declared war on Iraq. In response to Saddam Hussein's violent occupation of Kuwait, the USA sent a quick reaction force to Saudi to stop his army's advance. My unit was at Fort Hood, Texas, for six weeks of training before deploying to Saudi Arabia in support of Operation Desert Storm.

Nightly, US warplanes were bombing Iraqi ground forces as a part of our air campaign to free Kuwait. Televisions and computer screens were everywhere you turned, pumping in endless videos of the smallest details of the conflict. It was our first digital war.

We were in intense night training. Our mission that night was simple: fly west to an attack position and deliver simulated firepower against an imaginary enemy.

I would be leading this operation in an OH-58 Kiowa scout helicopter. Using ANVIS-6 night-vision goggles, we would fly low and fast without any lights. Two flights of armed AH-64 Apache gunship helicopters would be following me in formation flights. They would bring the firepower.

I zipped up my winter flight jacket against the cold and headed for my unit. I briefed my team in between sips of a hot cup of coffee.

'My aircraft will recon Route Delta in advance of two flights of AH-64 Apaches,' I described. 'They will be in tight formation flight three minutes apart. Charlie company will have two birds, Bravo company will have three. Once we reach our attack point, I will take up a rear over-watch position as the gunships deliver their munitions.'

We discussed important details and made sure everyone was on the same page. We synced our watches and went to work. Helicopter mechanics were crawling all over my bird, checking out every bolt and rivet.

'How's it going, McCoy?' I said to my enlisted flight observer, who would be flying right seat tonight. He was putting his gear into the back seat of our bird.

'I'm good, Lieutenant,' he said.

Sergeant Ronnie McCoy was a bright young soldier from Holly Springs, North Carolina. Quiet, but very sharp, he was always focused and an asset in the cockpit. I was glad he was with me that night. His presence boosted my confidence.

I was feeling the fatigue from several straight nights of intense night flying, but the coffee cleared my head. I heard

Staff Sergeant Roy Mitchell, my platoon sergeant, shout at the mechanics as they prepared my aircraft for the mission. Sergeant Mitchell was always on top of the little things. I trusted him. He took care of our aircraft as though they were his babies.

I went back over the mission one more time, tracing the route with my finger on the map on my kneeboard. Everything was clear in my mind. In many ways it was a routine mission . . . but this mission would be anything but routine.

I started the engine of my aircraft, feeling the familiar surge of adrenalin at the sound of that 420 horse-power turbine engine roaring to life. I always loved that sound. I smelled the familiar scent of burning jet fuel. It smelled like flying. I loved it.

Once I felt we were ready, I checked my watch: 8.15 pm. Time to roll.

I lowered my night-vision goggles over my eyes, spooled the engine up to full speed and lifted the aircraft off the grass. I hovered for a few seconds, then pointed it southwest, heading 240 degrees. It was go time.

In seconds we were at mission speed of 115 knots. Flying past some houses along our route, I noticed a distinct hazy light around a light pole in a field to my right. That was a bad sign. When the temperature outside gets cold and the amount of moisture in the air is high, fog can form. For this kind of flying, fog was not good at all.

I made a mental note. 'Pay attention,' I told myself. 'That could be trouble.'

The first fifteen minutes of the mission were normal. Flying at high speed just above the tree tops is intense, especially at night, but I'd spent hundreds of hours doing it. My training had prepared me. It felt comfortable and familiar.

West Texas is a wide-open territory with long, flat stretches of terrain mixed with steep hills and ridges. In the daytime, you can see tumbleweeds blowing steadily across the ground on windy days.

We crossed the ridgeline and started descending into the valley below when – *bam!* – everything went white. We'd flown into a thick fog bank and were lost in a dense sea of white.

I instantly lost all reference points of the ground, the horizon or how the aircraft was flying. My night-vision goggles were useless now. I was unable to make out any images in front of us. My chest tightened and I took a deep breath.

I had only seconds to respond properly. As calmly as I could, I leaned into all my hours of emergency training. I pulled in power to start the aircraft into a climb. In my head, I clicked through the emergency procedure for fog: maintain level flight, transition from visual flight to instrument flight, climb straight ahead above all known obstacles and maintain steady aircraft control until emerging from the fog.

I lifted my night-vision goggles and locked my eyes on the instruments. We were in a steady climb. I prayed a quick prayer.

All my focus was turned to those six key instruments on the cockpit dashboard: attitude indicator, airspeed indicator, altimeter, compass, VSI (vertical speed indicator) and fuel gauge. In instrument flight, those six instruments will tell you everything the aircraft is doing. They are truth, no matter what your body or your feelings are telling you.

After about twenty tense seconds, which felt like an hour, we popped out of the cloud bank into clear skies.

'Praise God!' burst from my lips. I felt the tightness in my chest release a little.

'Great,' McCoy said, in his usual quiet manner. He breathed
a deep sigh of relief. We were both on edge, but glad to be
free of the fog. Re-engaging my night-vision goggles, I could
see the stars, the horizon and the trees on the hills below us.
We were in the clear. Now we faced a new challenge.

Those two flights of Apaches were screaming along behind
us at 125 knots in tight formation flight. If they hit that fog
bank at that speed and that close together, a horrific collision
could occur.

We had seconds to contact the other aircraft. The mission
had to be aborted for safety. The lives of my fellow pilots were
in jeopardy. Our new task was to protect them from the
dangerous fog looming ahead.

I turned the aircraft left and started flying back towards
our unit base. I asked McCoy to dial up the frequency for
the flight leader of the first Apache formation. My heart
was pounding. The danger to my friends behind me was
screaming at me. They had no idea it was coming. I tried to
stay calm.

'Charlie 11, this is Charlie 06,' I said through my radio mic.
Then, 'Execute alpha,' I barked. 'I repeat, execute alpha. Do
you copy?' Execute alpha was code for 'mission abort'.

Instantly came the reply, 'Charlie 06, this is Charlie 11. I
understand execute alpha, is that correct?'

'Roger that, Charlie 11. Execute alpha, I repeat, execute
alpha,' I replied, my voice raised and intense.

'Roger, Charlie 06, executing alpha now,' he said calmly.
'Will contact Bravo 11 to execute alpha.'

In seconds, both Apache flights turned south and then east,
flying clear of the foggy danger we had struck.

I instantly felt a sense of peace that my buddies were safe.
I felt that the biggest crisis was behind me.

I was wrong.

There is one rule that is drilled into the heads of all pilots from their first day of flight training: fly the aircraft. No matter what happens inside or outside the helicopter, your main job is to fly the aircraft. 'Fly the aircraft' means to maintain control of the aircraft and stay aware of your surroundings. This is what will keep you alive and safe. Ignoring it can be fatal.

During those radio calls to my Apache pilot friends, I had committed the cardinal sin of all pilots: I had quit paying attention to flying the aircraft and had focused my attention on other things. I'd quit focusing on those six key instruments in front of me. It's easy to do in critical situations, but it can be deadly.

Other things were important in those moments, but the *most* important thing was to fly the aircraft. I'd lost my focus. Without realizing it, I had begun a slow, but steady, descent.

As I started thinking about my next radio call, I faintly heard McCoy say to me over the aircraft intercom, 'Lieutenant . . .'

'Not now, McCoy.' I brushed him off. 'Need to notify our battalion commander of this situation.'

My eyes were looking down towards my kneeboard, searching for our commander's call sign and radio frequency, when McCoy said it louder: 'Lieutenant!'

'McCoy, this is a critical situation. I need to . . .' My radio went blank.

McCoy had reached over and silenced my mic. He grabbed my right arm tightly and said it yet again, even louder: 'Lieutenant, look!' He pointed in front of our aircraft.

I looked up and my heart almost stopped in my chest. There, a few hundred feet in front of us, was the rocky face of a west Texas hill. We were seconds from becoming a crushed ball of flames. On collision course with that hill at over 100 miles an hour, we were at the point of facing certain death.

I quickly broke right and pulled in power, climbing up and away from the side of the mountain. We were clear.

The sight of that hill was like a blow to my brain. Something inside my head and heart went numb. I was stunned. I could hardly breathe.

'How could I have let that happen?!' I screamed inside. 'What was I thinking?'

Sergeant McCoy had saved us from death. His focus on the flight of our aircraft had kept us alive.

'I am so sorry, McCoy. I am so, so sorry,' I humbly coughed into my mic.

'It's OK, Lieutenant,' he said in relief. 'We made it.' I could hear his fear and caution starting to settle.

My attention now fully devoted to the right focus, I flew our bird safely back to base and landed without further incident. Once the skids of my aircraft had settled into the grass, I leaned my helmet against the cockpit instruments in front of me. I was exhausted.

'Oh, God, I can't believe what just happened,' I said to myself. And I started to imagine what could have taken place.

I thought about my family and how close I had come to never seeing them again. My pride had been shattered and my vulnerability as a pilot exposed. I would never be the same.

A few minutes later, I ducked into the operations tent and was met by the steely gaze of my commander, Lieutenant Colonel Mike Sawyer. I was embarrassed and visibly shaken. He put both his hands on my shoulders and looked into my eyes. He had heard it all unfold on the radio.

'Step outside with me, Lieutenant,' he said calmly. 'Tell me what happened out there.'

I told him everything. He nodded understandingly as he puffed on his trademark Cuban cigar.

'Yup,' he said. 'Got it.'

I wondered what he'd say next. I was afraid of the butt chewing I was about to receive.

'You saved the lives of a bunch of our pilots, Lieutenant,' he said firmly. 'Thank you.'

I couldn't believe what I was hearing.

'And you learned a valuable, critical lesson as a pilot,' he continued. 'Fly the aircraft. Always fly the aircraft. Focus on those instruments. They are your lifeline. Anyone who does what we do long enough will have one of these nights. You're just fortunate that you lived to tell about it.'

He smiled and took another drag on his cigar. 'Great job, son,' he said, slapping my left arm. 'Go get some rest.'

Areas of focus to thrive

Thriving takes focus. As we focus on the right things, we experience the grace of God supporting us and releasing momentum in our calling. The six principles of thriving are like the six instruments in my helicopter cockpit. Focus on them and you will move forward and get to where God is taking you.

Personal growth

1. *The Holy Spirit does the work of refining*
   (a) Relax, God's got this. Let grace work for you.
   (b) Cooperate with the Spirit and don't try to change yourself. Surrender to his work of convicting, comforting and empowering you in the refining process.

(c) Repent of any sin the Spirit brings to your attention and turn from it.

(d) Trust the Holy Spirit to lead you, guide you and transform you.

2. *Our true identity is the foundation of thriving*
   (a) Study God's Word concerning your place as his beloved son or daughter.
   (b) Reject the lies of the enemy over your identity. You are secure and favoured as God's child.
   (c) Write down some truths from God's Word or from the chapter on identity and speak them out loud over your life daily for a month.
   (d) If you've suffered from severe trauma in your life, pursue some deeper-level healing and prayer around your identity as a loved son or daughter. We often need others' help in finding wholeness after experiencing deep heart wounds.

3. *We thrive when we cooperate with our God-given design*
   (a) Don't worry about being like someone else. Celebrate your unique design.
   (b) Take a spiritual gifts test, Enneagram assessment or Gallup Strengthsfinder 2.0 assessment. Study the results carefully. Write down what you find. Look for patterns that indicate your design.
   (c) Study Romans 12:6–8 to find out which gifting/ wiring most reflects you and your personality. There are many online descriptions of these wirings. To hear a teaching on them, you can watch some videos we created here: <www.youtube.com/playlist?list= PLO5FNYoPFzsYE64zQzu2xAjUY68zwrxFD>.
   (d) Joyfully and unapologetically embrace your design and live from it. It will liberate you.

4. *Each of us has a sweet spot: the place we most naturally bear fruit*
   (a) Write down your deepest passions. Pray for God to make them clear to you.
   (b) Get a coach or find a coaching leader. Invest some time and resources in your own growth and development.
   (c) Look back over your life and write down all the times you felt the most alive and saw God work through you effectively to help others. Look for patterns that might indicate where your sweet spot is located. It's the intersection of your passion, wiring and fruit.
   (d) Do a time audit to determine what percentage of your work time is spent in your sweet spot. Increase the amount of time you're spending there. To learn more about a time audit, go to <https://tomcamacho.org> and click on Resources.

5. *The cross: God's great refining tool*
   (a) Embrace the pain that comes with the cross and death to self. Don't run from it.
   (b) Enlist the help of a loving coaching leader when you are in the midst of the flames of refining. God wants to do a work in you through it.
   (c) Cooperate with your coach and the Holy Spirit. They will help you come out on the other side, set free and not even smelling of smoke!

6. *All true thriving is relational*
   Draw near in your relationship with Jesus. He will fill you with his life. Your greatest investment is in people and your relationships. Study God's Word on how

healthy relationships work. Read books on boundaries and emotional health. Grow up in all aspects of your character so that you relate to others with the purity and love of Jesus.

Potential action steps to grow in Coaching Leadership at various levels

Personal level

1. Get a coach. Find a coach whom you trust and sign up for three to six months of coaching for your own personal growth. To request to be coached by myself, go to the Coaching tab on our website, <https://tomcamacho.org>, and click on Explore Coaching Options Now.

2. Study the six principles of Mining for Gold. Learn them and try them out for your own life.

3. Pray and ask God to show you some potential leaders in your local context or abroad. (Mining for Gold can happen using online tools such as Skype or Zoom from anywhere in the world where you have internet connection.)

4. Begin one-to-one Coaching Leadership meetings with key people in your context.

5. Practise the skills of Mining for Gold for six months. Evaluate the results. Ask the Holy Spirit how you can keep growing.

6. Attend our next Mining Workshop. Go to our website, <https://tomcamacho.org>, to sign up for our next Mining Workshop, where you as an individual will examine, with a group of other leaders, the deeper issues of the six principles of Mining for Gold.

7. Sign up for a Personal Leadership Retreat. Come away and dive into your own personal growth as a leader in the beautiful setting of the mountains of North Carolina. Go deep in examining your strengths, your passions, your dreams for the future and your leadership effectiveness. Go to <https://tomcamacho.org> to sign up.

Church level

1. Coaching Leadership works incredibly well in groups of three. Begin with small groups of three to twelve people who practise the Mining for Gold process with one another. With a group of three, one person is the coaching leader, the other is the coachee and the third is the prayer and feedback support person.
2. Start a church-wide small group series using the *Mining for Gold* book as a study resource. Break the groups into triplets to practise the Mining for Gold process.
3. Host an Empowering Leadership Workshop local training. Go to our coaching website at miningforgold.com to inquire about hosting a training with the leaders in your church or area of churches. Designate one or two coaches I can mentor before, during and after the training to serve as local experts in the Mining for Gold process.
4. Send some of your leaders to a Mining Workshop, Personal Leadership Retreat or Empowering Leadership Workshop to taste and see the power of the Mining for Gold paradigm. Check out tomcamacho.org for details.

In our journey to thriving, we must walk our own path; we must fly our own aircraft. We must maintain our own focus on the things that lead to life. No-one can do it for us. As coaching leaders, we must focus on the principles that lead to our own flourishing. Then we must lay down our lives to help as many other leaders as possible focus on the things that they need to thrive.

Final thoughts

I will end with the acrostic GOLD that we looked at earlier, which comprises the four core principles of Mining for Gold. Here are a few more encouragements for the future:

- *Gold is everywhere.* There is gold right under your feet. Take some time alone to be quiet before God. Just as Jesus did in Luke 6, pray to the Father and ask him who specifically he would have you invest in and develop. Pray to the Lord of the harvest to send you leaders you can develop as coaching leaders.
- *Open your eyes to see it.* Take time for some one-to-one coaching sessions with your current leaders. Ask the Holy Spirit to give you new eyes for them and faith for their development. Ask great questions and listen deeply to what they share with you. If some of them are stuck, take them through the six principles of thriving. Keep your eyes open as you interact with people on a daily basis. Listen to the Holy Spirit about who they are and what God might be doing in their lives. Invite them into a Coaching Leadership relationship for three to six months.
- *Learn the skills to draw it out.* Study what it means for leaders to thrive. Practise the principles of Mining for Gold. Take some time to read about coaching. If you find yourself passionate about coaching, attend coach

training and pursue a certification as a professional
coach. Learn how to ask great questions. Work on your
listening skills. Improve your discernment of where
and how the Holy Spirit is working in a leader's life.

- *Develop others continuously.* Be intentional about
  leadership development. Invest in key leaders around
  you. Equip others to learn to use the Mining for Gold
  tools. Host an Empowering Leadership Workshop, or
  send some of your leaders to our online Mining
  Workshop. Create an ongoing leadership development
  course in your local church.

The opportunity for kingdom impact through Coaching
Leadership is staggering. With these tools, we could see
thousands of leaders find their sweet spot and bear lasting
fruit in their local community. Don't hold back or play it safe.
Invest your best stuff in others. Give away everything to the
people who will be able to teach others too. Open up your
heart and your hands. Go change the world.

BIBLE ACKNOWLEDGMENTS